Photo Work:

Photo Work:

Forty Photographers on Process and Practice

Edited by Sasha Wolf

aperture

Table of Contents

Questionnaire

1. What comes first for you: the idea for a project, or individual photographs that suggest a concept?

2. What are the key elements that must be present for you when you are creating a body of work? (Social commentary, strong form, personal connection, photographic reference…)

3. Is the idea of a body of work important to you? How does it function in relation to making a great individual photograph?

4. Do you have what you might call a "photographic style"?

5. Where would you say your style falls on a continuum between completely intuitive and intellectually formulated?

6. Assuming you now shoot in what you would consider your natural voice, have you ever wished your voice was different?

7. How do you know when a body of work is finished?

8. Have you ever had a body of work that was created in the editing process?

9. Do you associate your work with a particular genre of photography? If yes, how would you define that genre?

10. Do you ever revisit a series that has already been exhibited or published to shoot more and add to it?

11. Do you ever revisit a series that has already been exhibited or published and *reedit* it?

12. Do you create with presentation in mind, be that a gallery show or a book?

Introduction

Sasha Wolf

The format of this book is simple. It is structured as a Proust-like questionnaire—meant to elicit personal, truthful insights—in which a wide range of photographers were each asked the same set of twelve questions, resulting in a typology of responses that allows for an intriguing and edifying compare and contrast. The questions are centered on the creation of a sustained body of work: How does a photographic project or series evolve? How important are the ideas of "style" and "genre"? What comes first, an individual photograph or a specific idea?

When I was putting this book together, one of the contributing artists told me that she felt the questions were very "intense." I'm not sure if she meant it as a compliment, but I took it as one! After all, I very intentionally set out to make something that is, above all else, truthful and authentic. I didn't want the participants to say what they thought they should say—I find that a bore—but, instead, to communicate how they really felt. The questions were designed to provoke honest, unvarnished responses—the "truth" about each individual's unique process of making work, specifically a body of work, rather than any one individual image. I also wanted to understand better how various photographers think about the work they've made once it's out in the world. My hope is that this book provides real world guidance in an area that is not typically approached from the practical side: the creative process. The questions are meant to invite answers that lean toward the matter-of-fact rather than the theoretical or philosophical. Having said that, once the participants were left to their own devices, some went on little tangent road-trips, and these meanderings, of course, turned out to be just as valuable and engaging as the concrete factoids.

My inspiration for the project came from hearing countless young photographers lament that they often feel adrift in their own practices; they wonder if they are doing it "right." They are nervous about the idea of creating a body of work with coherence, substance, and staying power. What one discovers, reading the wildly divergent responses from this group of photographers, both established and newly emerging, is that there is no single path. Instead, the reader is offered insight into the essentials of photographic practice from a wide range of perspectives.

The deeper motivation for making this book emerges from my own past life as a filmmaker. I appreciate many of the anxieties photographers face as they begin new projects. My experiences with the artists I've worked with over the years, as a gallerist, curator, and editor, have been extremely fulfilling due in no small part to the many ways in which I can relate to their struggles and successes. I am very sympathetic to the torture of the proverbial blank page: the ways that infinite options can be the greatest source of anguish.

One of the hardest things about being an artist is that there is no map to follow. You are like Lewis and Clark: you must draw your own. And that, of course, becomes a lot easier after you determine how the pencil feels most comfortable in your hand.

In truth, as we home in on our own unique way of seeing (born, in part, of who we are in the world), and figure out our best modus operandi, the seemingly endless set of options narrow, so that we slowly discover that we need not be paralyzed by infinite choices, but rather become gloriously aware of the handful of paths that truly suit each of us.

There are so many times an artist feels pressure to make a certain kind of work—often out of genuine admiration and appreciation. There are so many "shoulds" that go along with developing an artistic practice: what one finds out in listening to artists talk about their own processes is that each person has their own approach that has evolved over years of trial and error, and the trick is in finding out what works for you. For some photographers, the key is to get out and shoot, and the projects arise from the practice of being out in the world. For others, the first steps are taken internally—a set of questions or specific topics of interests to be pursued.

One can plainly appreciate, in looking at the list of contributing artists, that they are all connected to the loose grouping of "straight photography." Some, clearly, more than others, but all have some relationship to this approach. I felt it was important for the conceit of the book—the compare and contrast among the questions and answers—for the contributors to be working, more or less, within the same vein. Frankly, this is the type of photography I have championed throughout my career. That is to say, photographs that attempt to perfectly combine a view of the world that one may find familiar with the artist's inner life, creating then something new. As Robert Adams says in *Beauty in Photography: Essays in Defense of Traditional Values*, a book that has provided me with constant inspiration and guidance throughout my own career and, to be honest, one I loosely modeled this book after vis-à-vis its approachability and general warm heartedness:

Art asserts that nothing is banal, which is to say that a
serious landscape picture is metaphor. If a view of geography
does not imply something more enduring than a specific
piece of terrain, then the picture will hold us only briefly;
we will probably prefer the place itself, which we can smell
and feel and hear as well as see—though we are also likely
to come away from the actual scene hoping somewhere to
find it in art. This is because geography by itself is difficult
to value accurately—what we hope for from the artist is
help in discovering the significance of a place.

As I've gotten older I've come to appreciate how important the role
of a mentor is in the artist's life and how few artists have access to
one, especially once they leave school. I hope that this book can serve
the function of a mentor in its own way, offering guidance to some,
validation to others, and perhaps even a few lightning bolts to those
photographic artists who have all the tools they need—and are just
struggling to figure out how to employ them. And one last thought:
in reading over all of the contributions, it's become abundantly clear
to me that this book will be illuminating and entertaining for other
categories of people as well, from artists of other mediums to art
collectors and art lovers. It's just a lot of fun! ◑

"Categories are mostly useful to curators and historians. For artists they tend to be cages."

Robert Adams

First camera:
Miranda 35 mm SLR

First meaningful photobook:
Long before I ever thought about being a photographer, my sister gave me a copy of *The Family of Man* (edited by Edward Steichen, 1955), which I loved for both the pictures and the quotations.

Robert Adams (born in Orange, New Jersey, 1937) is a recipient of a MacArthur Fellowship, two Guggenheim Fellowships, the Spectrum International Prize for Photography (1995), the Deutsche Börse Photography Prize (2006), and the Hasselblad Foundation International Award in Photography (2009). In 2014, he was elected to the American Academy of Arts and Letters. His books include *From the Missouri West* (Aperture, 1980), *Beauty in Photography: Essays in Defense of Traditional Values* (Aperture, 1981), *Our Lives and Our Children: Photographs Taken Near the Rocky Flats Nuclear Weapons Plant 1979–1983* (1983, reissued 2016), *Summer Nights* (Aperture, 1985), *Why People Photograph: Selected Essays and Reviews* (Aperture, 1994), *Summer Nights, Walking* (Aperture and Yale University Art Gallery, 2009), and *The Question of Hope: Photographs in Western Oregon* (2013). Adams earned a PhD in English from the University of Southern California in 1965. He lives in Oregon.

First meaningful exhibition:
Because I lived at the edge of the world, the first meaningful exhibition I saw was of my own work, together with Emmet Gowin's, at MoMA, in 1971.

Personal fact:
In high school I played the lead in a stage production of *Lost Horizon*. Alas, my wife Kerstin now admits to having difficulty imagining me as Ronald Colman, the actor who played the part in the movie (1937)!

1. What comes first for you: the idea for a project, or individual photographs that suggest a concept?

> Thinking up a project and then making pictures that fit does not, in my experience, usually result in the best pictures. Most of the books I've published have started with just walking and photographing, free of any plan.

2. What are the key elements that must be present for you when you are creating a body of work? (Social commentary, strong form, personal connection, photographic reference...)

> All of those factors can be compelling, but mostly I need to love what I see (which may include, of course, objecting to its destruction). I think it was Simone Weil who said that prayer is complete attention. That's pretty close.

3. Is the idea of a body of work important to you? How does it function in relation to making a great individual photograph?

> When I'm looking through the finder I'm trying to discover form and wholeness in the specific view in front of me. Though I do carry with me a recollection of what I and other picture-makers have done before in similar circumstances.

4. Do you have what you might call a "photographic style"?

> Not unless respect qualifies as a style. My goal is not to make a fashion statement or an investment opportunity.

5. Where would you say your style falls on a continuum between completely intuitive and intellectually formulated?

> Style again. Let's be clear: the effort that's worth making is to try to create helpful, lasting photographs, what Dorothea Lange called "second lookers." We're not talking about how to plot career moves in pursuit of name recognition, gallery representation, or money. Though having said that, photographers have to eat, and I'm sympathetic with those who face difficulties. This is America, after all—a savage place.

6. Assuming you now shoot in what you would consider your natural voice, have you ever wished your voice was different?

> I admire portraits by Judith [Joy] Ross, and sometimes I wish I could make pictures like hers. But I can't. Nor, of course, can I play the viola de gamba like Jordi Savall. It just isn't going to happen.

7. How do you know when a body of work is finished?

> I'm never completely sure, but at some point the subject seems convincingly explored, its complexities acknowledged.

8. Have you ever had a body of work that was created in the editing process?

> No. But you surely can *un*make a body of good pictures with poor editing. Editing is every bit as hard as making photographs. No two pictures are qualitatively equal. Their proper ordering cannot be determined by rule. And, there is often the difficulty of deciding whether a picture should be included at all. Is it faithful to the subject? Some of the problem is in freeing yourself from the memory of standing there when you took the photograph, amazed and hopeful and trying hard. It's the same struggle that Flannery O'Connor said a writer faces: "The writer has to judge himself with a stranger's eye and a stranger's scrutiny."

9. Do you associate your work with a particular genre of photography? If yes, how would you define that genre?

> Categories are mostly useful to curators and historians. For artists they tend to be cages.

10. Do you ever revisit a series that has already been exhibited or published to shoot more and add to it?

> Yes. No subject is ever completely used up. I take heart from the fact that it's nearly impossible to shoot exactly the same picture on succeeding days. More broadly, life's joys and sorrows remain more or less the same, so we can and should revisit them. Freshly, of course, avoiding clichés.
>
> Relatedly, no other photographer has a monopoly on a subject. You can still shoot a pepper. I once even had the temerity to photograph the church at Hernandez [New Mexico]. The result was not, to say the least,

competition for Ansel Adams's masterpiece, but it was different, and—do I dare say it?—not uninteresting.

11. Do you ever revisit a series that has already been exhibited or published and *reedit* it?

Yes. With the help of many good people I've reedited and republished a number of books. The originals suffered from smaller budgets and now outmoded printing technologies, and I'd excluded some effective pictures and included some weaker ones.

12. Do you create with presentation in mind, be that a gallery show or a book?

Ah, a question for comic relief! I've never struggled to make a picture and at the same time worried about which kind of molding I'd like for a frame.

Am I permitted to close with something serious, even though it only speaks to an issue that seems to be behind the stated questions? Flannery O'Connor lived to be only thirty-nine years old, but her advice was unambiguous: "Be properly scared and go on doing what you have to do." ◑

Dawoud Bey

First camera:
Argus C3 rangefinder, which I
received from my godmother

First meaningful photobook:
The Sweet Flypaper of Life (1955) by
Roy DeCarava and Langston Hughes

Dawoud Bey (born in New York, 1953) earned his MFA from Yale
University School of Art (1993). He is a professor of photography
at Columbia College Chicago, where he began teaching in 1998,
and served as the 2008–10 Distinguished College Artist. Bey
has received several awards, including National Endowment for
the Arts grants, a Guggenheim Fellowship, and a MacArthur
Fellowship. Among his published works are *Dawoud Bey:
Portraits 1975–1995* (1995), *The Chicago Project* (2003), *Class
Pictures* (Aperture, 2007), *Picturing People* (2012), *Harlem, USA*
(2012), *The Birmingham Project* (2013), *Dawoud Bey: Seeing
Deeply* (2018), and *Dawoud Bey on Photographing People and
Communities* (The Photography Workshop series, Aperture, 2019).

First meaningful exhibition:
Harlem on My Mind (1969) at the
Metropolitan Museum of Art

1. What comes first for you: the idea for a project, or individual photographs that suggest a concept?

> My work always begins with an idea, with something that I need to talk about. I make my photographs in order to provoke a conversation around those things that I am invested in. The challenge is how to give those concerns a resonant and coherent form so that the viewer becomes interested and invested. I want the things that matter to me to matter to the viewer.

2. What are the key elements that must be present for you when you are creating a body of work? (Social commentary, strong form, personal connection, photographic reference…)

> I think the main thing is that each individual photograph has to function in a way that compels a viewer to want to engage with it. Making photographs, for me, is always about how one uses the visual poetics of picture-making and then weds that notion to a meaningful intention and subject. So, I want each photograph within a project to compel the viewer's attention . . . through the use of form, color, light, tonality, vantage point, and the other devices that I have at my disposal. All of those things are deployed in the interest of creating an engagement with the subject, whether a person, a community, or a history.

3. Is the idea of a body of work important to you? How does it function in relation to making a great individual photograph?

> I've never made random photographs, except when I was very young and was trying to figure out what my subject would be. I have pretty much always thought of my projects as the making of a particular body of work. Early on, the desire to reconnect with the Harlem community of my mother and father and to challenge stereotypical representations of black urban subjects led to a five-year exploration of that community. That became my first completed project, Harlem, USA. That project was also about my desire to be in conversation with the history of how Harlem has been visualized, and to contribute something to the art and culture that has come out of and been produced in that community.

4. Do you have what you might call a "photographic style"?

> With each project, I have consciously set out to find a visual language that makes sense for that particular project. I've never wanted to

become my own oldies show, so I've never worried about a consistent style. I think I take my cues from musicians I respect in that regard. Miles Davis's music always evolved, and he chafed at those listeners who wanted him to maintain the style he helped define in the 1940s, '50, and '60s. What I think is consistent throughout my work is the desire to see deeply into the subject. With the portraits, that meant making photographs that suggest the rich interior life of the subjects, not just their surface appearances.

Over the more than forty years that I've been making photographs, I've made pictures working in the street, initially with a handheld 35 mm camera and black-and-white material, and then a tripod-mounted 4-by-5 camera with a Polaroid back and Type 55 positive/negative film; then I moved into the studio and spent eight years making color photographs, using the 20-by-24 Polaroid View Camera, with lights and backdrops. After that, I went back to the 4-by-5 and color material, and more recently a tripod-mounted 6-by-7 camera, and now a handheld 6-by-7 camera. I do think my work is as much about exploring the possibilities of picture-making as it is about the subjects I'm interested in.

5. Where would you say your style falls on a continuum between completely intuitive and intellectually formulated?

I've worked both ways, and made meaningful work deploying very different strategies. So it really depends on the work that I am in the midst of.

6. Assuming you now shoot in what you would consider your natural voice, have you ever wished your voice was different?

Whenever I've wanted to use a different voice, I've changed the tools I use to make my work. It keeps me from falling into an overly comfortable set of habits, and gives me a new set of challenges to confront.

7. How do you know when a body of work is finished?

On the one hand, I think the project is finished when I have said visually all that I think needs to be said about that particular subject. But one never knows. Recently I thought my project Harlem Redux [published in 2012] was done, but then I started to feel like there were gaps in terms of the kinds of pictures, range of subjects, and varying vantage points from which I wanted to tell the story about the ways in which the Harlem community is changing. I couldn't shake this nagging feeling that there was more to do, and so I went back. Turns out, I made some of the strongest photographs on that visit. So sometimes you know, and sometimes you don't.

8. Have you ever had a body of work that was created in the editing process?

No. I have no idea how that might work. The project for me is made deliberately from picture to picture, being mindful that I need to keep mixing up the picture-making strategies so I don't end up with a bunch of photographs that look the same in some conspicuous way, even as they need to hold together as a group. I am kind of editing even as I'm out in the world. While I'm working I try to develop the film, make proof prints, and then larger prints as quickly as possible. I need to be able to see what I'm doing so I can continue to shape the project in a way that is continually expansive. Part of what makes the work cohere is that I have always used only one lens on my camera so that there is a consistent visual "look" or field of vision.

9. Do you associate your work with a particular genre of photography? If yes, how would you define that genre?

I let others worry about genres. I always tell my students, I only know of two kinds of photographs: interesting ones and uninteresting ones. Very often genre is merely a matter of context—ie, whether the work is published in a magazine or a newspaper, or hung in a museum or a gallery. Throughout the history of the medium there have been lots of photographs that have migrated from one context into another.

10. Do you ever revisit a series that has already been exhibited or published to shoot more and add to it?

No.

11. Do you ever revisit a series that has already been exhibited or published and *reedit* it?

No.

12. Do you create with presentation in mind, be that a gallery show or a book?

My work exists primarily in museums and galleries. When I'm making the work that's the context I'm thinking about: how it's going to look on the wall, what size the prints should be, how they will "hold the wall." Museum spaces tend to be larger, and so that creates a different conversation than would happen if the work were on the printed page.

With my Class Pictures project I knew I wanted the work ultimately to be published as a book [2007], but even before it was published it was seen in a series of exhibitions in each of the cities where the work was made. So I always visualize my work in an exhibition context as I am making it; that's where I know it's destined to be seen. For me, the work is completed once it's on the wall. ◑

"The more layers a project has, the more possibility there is that one of those layers will relate to someone."

Alejandro Cartagena

First camera:
I bought a Minolta 35 mm while working as a front-desk clerk at a hotel in Austin, Texas.

First meaningful photobook:
Uncommon Places: The Complete Works (2004) by Stephen Shore

Mexican photographer **Alejandro Cartagena** (born in Santo Domingo, Dominican Republic, 1977) lives and works in Monterrey, Mexico. Cartagena is a recipient of a Photolucida Critical Mass Book Award and a Premio IILA–FotoGrafia Award in Rome. He has self-published and had published award-winning books, among them *Carpoolers* (2014), *Before the War* (2015), *Headshots* (2015), *Rivers of Power* (2016), *Santa Barbara Return Jobs to US* (2016), *Santa Barbara Shame on US* (2017), and *A Guide to Infrastructure and Corruption* (2017).

First meaningful exhibition:
Erwin Wurm's solo show at La Fototeca de Nuevo León in Monterrey, Mexico. As part of the installation crew, at the end I got to destroy some of the huge exhibition prints.

Personal fact:
I like to talk to my plants about my trips and my feelings.

1. What comes first for you: the idea for a project, or individual photographs that suggest a concept?

It has happened both ways. I have been obsessed for years with finding new projects to work on. As I read, travel, or surf the web, I always think of the possibilities. That has taken me to many of the projects I have done and continue to do today. At times, I have purposely let go of that frame of mind and gone with, what I would tell myself, is the pleasure of just taking pictures. Sometimes it has worked out, sometimes it hasn't.

I still feel a need to have an umbrella idea with which to work, even if I don't know exactly what I'll photograph. I guess because of the in-depth research and reading I do for the subjects I've worked with, it is hard to leave the conceptual part of my creative process. I don't think it's a problem if you know it's there. Right now, my newest work is with vintage and archival images, working with the physicality of the photograph. Though now there is a thread to all this new work, it was more intuitive at the beginning as I didn't know exactly how the images would look until after the manipulations occurred. This has brought back a feeling of uncertainty that was very present at the beginning of my career when I never knew exactly what would result.

2. What are the key elements that must be present for you when you are creating a body of work? (Social commentary, strong form, personal connection, photographic reference…)

I think in layers. The more layers a project has, the more possibility there is that one of those layers will relate to someone. Something like this: the project needs to be aesthetically, technically, conceptually, and historically relevant; have a personal connection; pull toward some kind of social commentary; be able to show personal and artistic vulnerability; and so on. Some of the layers are just sparks of interest that will allow a later reading of what I am trying to present as subject matter or theme. Certain viewers will be interested in the technical aspects of the work, to start, and expectantly move into the other layers of meaning, history, or narrative involved in the book, exhibition, or site. I feel something worthy happens when one of these layers is perceived, and I also hope that people will find more of the threads that are offered, though I never know if that will happen. In the end, my own personal commitment is to make the work as layered as possible, and in doing so, I also make the best work I think I can do.

3. Is the idea of a body of work important to you? How does it function in relation to making a great individual photograph?

> I feel that for me it has always been about a body of work. I love individual photographs, but I feel really attracted to a narrative that builds up from parts or a theme that is constructed through repetitions or seriality. I guess it is a very pragmatic way of seeing how photography works in that if you insist on what is represented (typologies) or fix the sequence through a book, the meanings seem to float out of the work in an easier way. Maybe. There are still codes that don't really mean anything outside the photography world. Sometimes I do question this way of working, but that is the vulnerability you have to decide to show: that you think in a certain way, you believe in something, and that both things will be questioned. That seems exciting to me.

4. Do you have what you might call a "photographic style"?

> I feel I work with styles more than having a style I am trapped in. I use styles to produce sensations that help my subjects. It is another layer of meaning I can consciously think of once I am putting together the body of work, maybe at the beginning or even during the production. It isn't always that conscious, but once I get a feel of how the style helps the work "work" then I make decisions as to whether to continue that route or switch to something that functions better for the project. I've used many camera formats, film sizes, and presentations, and I always try the style that is in service to the meaning of the work, and not the other way around. But it's not the only way I will work in the future. Form and style can be interesting as they are, and that attracts me too.

5. Where would you say your style falls on a continuum between completely intuitive and intellectually formulated?

> It depends on the project. It is very intuitive, and I am open to going either way. I really enjoy other people's projects that are just the idea, but I also love good messy projects that don't seem to go anywhere. I want to do both things.

6. Assuming you now shoot in what you would consider your natural voice, have you ever wished your voice was different?

> I think I've had moments where that voice has been overwhelming and has made me stay in the limits of the ideas and styles of what

projects I've done and how I've produced them. I think now if there is such a voice in my work, it has to do with creating things that excite me and make me wonder about unknown areas, so there is always new stuff happening. This year I've done a risograph book of found photographs and started doing collages from my previous works; I'm cutting up photographs while at the same time I'm doing medium- and large-format photographs of a long-term project I've been working on for the past seven years.

7. How do you know when a body of work is finished?

It depends, but I do force myself to finish and close by publishing a book or zine or doing an exhibition. I see unfinished works as ghosts that come into other projects and don't let you move forward because you're always thinking of what else you can do to make the project better or what it's still missing. A body of work is finished when you decide it is finished. That is how I feel about it.

8. Have you ever had a body of work that was created in the editing process?

Yes. This kind of goes back to the earlier question of what comes first, the idea for a project or the individual photographs. I think it can happen both ways in the editing process, too. I've had a book "happen" through editing. The meaning or the theme came through the sequence and editing of the work into a photobook. Authorship seems to me very related to the editing process. It isn't enough nowadays to just have great images; you need to somehow put those images into a sequence, narrative, or group to make them go somewhere else than just "these are great." Or maybe not! For me, it is again the layers idea. I'll have great images, edit and sequence them in the best possible way, produce a beautiful book (or exhibition) that is physically connected in scale and materials to the subject matter, and through the sum of all these parts, you'll have a work of art. If any part of the process falls short, the project will suffer.

9. Do you associate your work with a particular genre of photography? If yes, how would you define that genre?

> I think I would consider most of my works to be of the documentary genre, but I don't feel stuck in it. I think documentary today has become broadened because of photobooks and the possibilities to create narratives more than specific stories. Documentary for me is about the idea of looking into things that have occurred in the world and creating a project that is openly subjective without the pretense that it is telling the truth; it is a particular point of view and not the whole story. I mean, documentary films are pure montage, no? They are moving images of real people and places, but there is a storyboard and an editing process to make the movie attractive to watch. I want documentary photography to do that too.

10. Do you ever revisit a series that has already been exhibited or published to shoot more and add to it?

> I try not to. Like I said before, they can become ghosts, and it can get messy. I do think about the images that I could have done, but it is just a game; I try not to spend time actually doing more images for closed projects. I do, however, like going back to look at images that weren't used to see if there could be another project for those images. The distance time offers can open up new veins for how to address the subject. Some of my books, like *Before the War* [2015], are clear examples of this. The original project was about the state of Nuevo León [Mexico], its sites and peoples, but years after taking those images I realized how those places were where the drug war had started, but naively I hadn't even felt that during the two years I was traveling there. Through the eyes of an editor, I was able to jump over the original idea and look for things that were referencing the drug war. The experiment was a bit nerve-racking because I had to let go of why I had originally done the images, but the results were, in my mind, better than the original project.

11. Do you ever revisit a series that has already been exhibited or published and *reedit* it?

> I think I kind of went there with the last answer, but I'll give another example of what I've done with this revisiting practice. For the *Carpoolers* book I had a whole year of editing before I felt I had something worth showing. It would still take three more finished dummies until we came

to a final book. We went to press for the first edition [2014], and since then my editor and I have gone back to reedit the book three times. There are always things you miss or don't see when editing. Since I've self-published the book, it has been easy to go back and do a new book each time; format, sequence, and images change in all three. Why spend time and money copy and pasting a book from one edition to the next?

12. Do you create with presentation in mind, be that a gallery show or a book?

It depends on the project. I've done it both ways, but I also just do the work for the work's sake: because it's fun, because I'm curious about the subject, or just because I found photographs of something that interests me and I start playing around with them with no purpose at all. I do have to say that having a final presentation in mind has made me accelerate the production and editing process. ◑

Elinor Carucci

First camera:
My father's old Canon

First meaningful photobook:
The Ballad of Sexual Dependency
(1986) by Nan Goldin

Elinor Carucci (born in Jerusalem, 1971) graduated in 1995 from Bezalel Academy of Arts and Design with a degree in photography and moved to New York that same year. She has been awarded an International Center of Photography Infinity Award, a Guggenheim Fellowship, and a New York Foundation for the Arts fellowship. Carucci has published four monographs to date: *Closer* (2002), *Diary of a Dancer* (2005), *Mother* (2013), and *Midlife* (2019). She teaches in the graduate photography program at the School of Visual Arts.

First meaningful exhibition:
Growing up, I spent a lot of time at the Israel Museum in Jerusalem; my childhood memories blend it into one big meaningful exhibition/ environment/place that is so much a part of the reason why I became an artist.

Personal Fact:
I was a professional belly dancer for fifteen years.

1. What comes first for you: the idea for a project, or individual photographs that suggest a concept?

> Somehow both things are happening: I can have an idea for a project and then take individual pictures that will lead me to change the project. Many times I will take pictures that I think are about one thing, but they end up being about another thing—then I listen to my own pictures and understand what my project is about. At that point, I have the idea for a project that I follow and develop.

2. What are the key elements that must be present for you when you are creating a body of work? (Social commentary, strong form, personal connection, photographic reference…)

> The key elements: going from micro to macro; starting with the most personal, intimate, and familiar in order to talk about universal issues, issues that are at the very core of who we are as human beings, our emotions, feelings, relationships; the microcosm of the family that contains the basis for every other connection to behavior in our lives.

3. Is the idea of a body of work important to you? How does it function in relation to making a great individual photograph?

> The idea of a body of work is very important to me. It's what leads me to create the specific images I make, leads me to want to create them. It's the umbrella that allows me to grow and develop and add and change.

4. Do you have what you might call a "photographic style"?

> Yes. I have a style that has grown and developed over the years. It was mostly created intuitively at first, but then later on it developed when I recognized certain elements in my work that I loved and others I wanted to get rid of.

5. Where would you say your style falls on a continuum between completely intuitive and intellectually formulated?

> Some days on one end of the spectrum, other days on the other, and the rest of the days in between. The style is also determined by crucial decisions done by editing, what goes out, what stays, what is being worked on in Photoshop, what is printed and how, sizes, and

sequencing. All those decisions range from the very intuitive and emotional to the rational and intellectual.

6. Assuming you now shoot in what you would consider your natural voice, have you ever wished your voice was different?

No.

7. How do you know when a body of work is finished?

With some bodies of work I know because they follow a certain period in my life that has ended. *Diary of a Dancer* [2005] ended because I got pregnant and was not performing anymore. It was the end of what would have been my life as a full-time professional belly dancer, and had there been a few more years it might have made for a better book, but this is life, and sometimes things finish before you have enough good pictures. However, the fact that it took years to find a publisher for *Closer* [2002] made it a better book; a decade of picture-making was necessary for it to feel like a decade in time. With *Mother* [2013], the project ended when I began to feel that my children were growing apart from me, and that the period in my life when, to me, the three of us felt like we were one unit was changing. Ending. It was so hard to acknowledge it. Hard to call it a finished project.

8. Have you ever had a body of work that was created in the editing process?

No. They are made while being photographed, and then tweaked, slightly changed, and hopefully made better, in the process of editing.

9. Do you associate your work with a particular genre of photography? If yes, how would you define that genre?

I don't because I refuse to. I think that identifying genres is necessary for the market of photography and art but can be damaging to the artist.

Let's take, for example, the words *fine art photography*. I see art in many forms of photography: I see it in war photography, documentary photography, fashion photography, magazine photography. And many times I go to galleries to look at what I think will be art and recognize commercial ways of thinking, pieces being made in order to be used as decoration, in order to fit into trends that happen to be appreciated at the moment, in order to be sellable.

I am making art. It is sometimes staged and sometimes a snapshot, sometimes conceptual and sometimes emotional, and sometimes, if I am lucky enough, both. Who cares. Fuck the genre.

Art is when we can go deeper, and think, and feel, and understand, and analyze. And laugh and cry. And then go even a little deeper.

10. Do you ever revisit a series that has already been exhibited or published to shoot more and add to it?

Yes. I feel I learn from each exhibition, each book, each magazine portfolio, the many talks I give about my work, every time I write more about a specific body of work. And then there is life . . . I grow older and things I thought I finished photographing continue to grow. I find myself discovering more, surprised by some images when I realize they are a continuation of an older body of work.

Some examples are the work I did with my husband in *Closer* and in the project Crisis [2001–3], then in the last couple of years, and probably in the future. Our marriage continues to change, more layers are being added to our relationship, we've had children, we've grown older. I might continue to revisit this "project" until the day I die.

11. Do you ever revisit a series that has already been exhibited or published and *reedit* it?

Yes, yes, I feel that the editing and revising can continue forever, because I grow and change all the time, and so the way I see my own work, and edit it, will forever continue to change if the opportunity to reedit occurs.

12. Do you create with presentation in mind, be that a gallery show or a book?

No. I create with a story in mind to tell, a message to give. I tell the whole story at the end of a project.

Then I will adjust the story, maybe show some parts of it, maybe a fraction of it, maybe the whole thing, according to the avenue I am putting it into: a group show, a small solo show, a big solo show, a book. ❍

John Chiara

First camera:
When I was nine, in 1980, I received a Nikon FE and several rolls of color film for Christmas. The FE had been introduced a few years earlier and included an aperture-priority setting, so it would select the correct shutter speed according to what you chose as the aperture.

First meaningful photobook:
Rule Without Exception (1990) by Lewis Baltz. I ran across it in 1993. It is one of my favorite books of all time.

John Chiara (born in San Francisco, 1971) received a BFA in photography from the University of Utah in 1995 and an MFA in photography from the California College of the Arts in 2004. He was an artist in residence at Crown Point Press, San Francisco, in 2006 and 2017; Gallery Four, Baltimore, in 2010; Headlands Center for the Arts, Marin County, California, in 2010; and Budapest Art Factory in 2017 and 2019. His first publication *California* (Aperture/Pier 24 Photography) was published in 2017. Chiara lives in San Francisco.

First meaningful exhibition:
In 1988 our high school photography class went to see a group photography show at the San Francisco Museum of Modern Art. It was the first time I had been to a museum of this kind and was able to see in person high quality enlarged prints. I was excited by the sharp grain and richness of the contrast in Emmet Gowin's photographs of Matera, Italy.

1. What comes first for you: the idea for a project, or individual photographs that suggest a concept?

> The idea for a project comes first. Because I focus on making photographs for contemporary art exhibitions, the project is normally born out of an opportunity to work and exhibit in a particular region. This way of working allows me the time to explore the land and experiment with how I want to photograph it. As I work and find the photographs, I am always trying to visualize the work ahead of me and get a better sense of the exhibition to come. With that said, the concepts are solidified by experimentation and the making of the individual photographs.

2. What are the key elements that must be present for you when you are creating a body of work? (Social commentary, strong form, personal connection, photographic reference…)

> I usually seek out places with a rich history of depiction. I can spend years working in a particular region, developing a personal connection to it. I use photography to learn about and become intimate with my surroundings.
>
> I often spend my time observing what is around me, while thinking about the photographic medium. I also think about how others, in any medium, have depicted a place previously. I consider how those depictions make use of the notion of identity and how the collective memory of these depictions can lead to a sense of place. I try to explore that sense of place by digging into the area's history and thinking about the forces that shaped it, while also thinking about the history of photography itself. I hope to contribute to the collective photographic memory, which I see as inherent in the work that has been made in a region.
>
> On a more practical level, given the amount of equipment and just the physical side of the process, I really have to consider whether I'll be able to exhibit where I'm working and whether I'll have support to work there.

3. Is the idea of a body of work important to you? How does it function in relation to making a great individual photograph?

> Yes, it's a very important, driving theme. Images play off of each other and speak to each other. As this happens, I will start to get a sense of the other images that should be added to bolster the overarching feeling of where the work is headed.

I learn from each photograph I take. I only take a few on any given day. The setup and act of taking photographs is a slow process, and it can be days or even weeks before I develop them. This gives me ample time to think about what I did, which is aided by taking careful notes for each exposure. This process develops my intuition and my sense for photography. It is one of the main forces driving the direction of my work. It frames the window my curiosities can peer through.

4. Do you have what you might call a "photographic style"?

I have developed a process that is part photography, part sculpture, and part event. It is an undertaking that requires constant ingenuity and patience with the tools I use. I create one-of-a-kind photographs using a variety of hand-built cameras, the largest of which is a 50-by-80-inch field camera obscura that I move on a flatbed trailer. Once I select a location, I situate and then physically enter the camera, maneuvering in near total darkness a sheet of color photographic paper onto the camera's back wall. Throughout each exposure, I intuitively control the light entering the lens by using my hands to burn and dodge the projected image on the back wall. Later, back in the studio, I will develop the image in a spinning drum by agitating the chemistry over the paper lining the inside of the drum. I welcome aspects of the photographic event to be recorded, wherein the result is simultaneously an image, an object, and a document.

I hope to make photographs that are strongly perceptual and elicit a visceral response but where the viewer returns to the materiality of the photograph due to its mirrorlike qualities and divergent edges.

5. Where would you say your style falls on a continuum between completely intuitive and intellectually formulated?

More on the intuitive end, but my intuition has only been able to flourish through years of experience and taking detailed notes. In essence, I know what boundaries to set up for myself to operate within. I follow a train of thought as opposed to deciding beforehand, "This is what it's going to be." It's not thesis-driven.

6. Assuming you now shoot in what you would consider your natural voice, have you ever wished your voice was different?

No. I've found my voice through all my years of experimenting.

7. How do you know when a body of work is finished?

It's so hard to know! Maybe when I've run out of things to say and pictures I want to take. There are, of course, lots of practical and pragmatic reasons it ends: deadlines, energy, inspiration, resources. Even so, I find it very difficult to end a body of work. I might not ever truly end it because of the way I work. I can spend five or six years in a place if I'm drawn to it, even after an exhibition has ended. I revisit places. I continue following the train of thought until I feel it's resolved.

8. Have you ever had a body of work that was created in the editing process?

No, not really, because that's not how my process works. But we did just go through and edit down eighteen years of photos for my book *California* [2017]. You might say the body of work in the book form was "made" in the editing. The way I think of a body of work is also about the context in which it appears.

9. Do you associate your work with a particular genre of photography? If yes, how would you define that genre?

No. Maybe landscape photography, but a lot of my work is about photography itself.

10. Do you ever revisit a series that has already been exhibited or published to shoot more and add to it?

Yes. All the time. As I mentioned above, I will revisit a place for years.

11. Do you ever revisit a series that has already been exhibited or published and *reedit* it?

No.

12. Do you create with presentation in mind, be that a gallery show or a book?

Yes. For gallery exhibitions, I like to know where the work will be exhibited and create work with that in mind, often making more work than can be shown. For a book, the concept is in my mind, but not at the forefront. ◑

Kelli
Connell

First meaningful photobook:
In the summer of 1996, as a break from the Texas heat, I spent countless hours lying on the floor of a good friend's apartment poring over piles of photography books. Page by page, we fell in love with Larry Sultan's *Pictures from Home* (1992); were shocked, yet fascinated, by Larry Clark's *Tulsa* (1971); and were enthralled by *William Eggleston's Guide* (1976). We devoured images by Diane Arbus and Lee Friedlander. Yet the book that I found myself returning to the most was *Francesca Woodman: Photographic Works* (1993).

Kelli Connell (born in Oklahoma City, 1974) received a BFA in photography from University of North Texas, Denton (1997), and an MFA in photography from Texas Woman's University, Denton (2003). Her publications include the monograph *Kelli Connell: Double Life* (2011) and the forthcoming *Pictures for Charis*. Her work is featured in the three-volume anthology *MP3: Midwest Photographers Publication Project* (Aperture/Museum of Contemporary Photography, 2006). She lives in Chicago.

Personal fact:
It's always fun to have Kiba Jacobson, the model in *Double Life*, attend an opening reception because most people assume my images are self-portraits. I get to sit back, comfortable with my invisibility, and watch the scenario unfold.

1. What comes first for you: the idea for a project, or individual photographs that suggest a concept?

For me, a loose idea for a project comes first, and then individual photographs start to shape this concept into something that I don't always expect. For example, the photographs that I made before I landed on what is now the project Double Life [published in book form in 2011] included composites of my model Kiba Jacobson seen multiple times, sometimes as many as ten times, in each scene. This was too surreal for the work. It wasn't until I constructed an image that depicted only two of her that I realized that this approach was much more in line with what I wanted to communicate in a larger body of work. That first image, entitled *Giggle*, depicts two young women on a couch laughing together. I noticed that the work could be read on multiple levels. On the one hand, it could be read as a relationship between two people, and on the other hand, it could be interpreted as the relationship that we have with ourselves.

I began making photographs for Double Life at a time when I was newly single. I was questioning my own sexuality and the roles that I had played in past relationships. By casting the same model to play both characters in a relationship, or as two sides of the self, I was able to raise questions about the roles we assume in regard to gender, sexuality, and identity.

So, working with only two characters in each scene allowed for a more complex reading of the work while also calling into question the veracity of the photograph. These photographs look like documentary images. Yet they are completely constructed. I believe that some of our most private thoughts are very real to us and working in this way allows me to create a visual truth, or document, of these interior investigations as something tangible, as an image on a piece of paper. For me, photography has been the perfect medium to explore these ideas. As the project has evolved over time, it has been important for me to create images that are not repetitive. I began to make images that were more complicated technically. I also made sure to examine my own life experiences that have naturally evolved over time. I began this work in my late twenties and continued it in my thirties, and now into my forties. Now that my model is in her forties as well it has become even more important for me that her body is represented in the art world, a sphere where far too often women over forty are not recognized.

2. What are the key elements that must be present for you when you are creating a body of work? (Social commentary, strong form, personal connection, photographic reference...)

> I strive for a complex reading of my work. It is really hard for me to take one picture and think that it is finished. So, creating layers of meaning within a single image is something that is important. And if these layers of meaning have a hierarchy, top on the list is the emotional tone. In Double Life, I want viewers to be consumed by the sexual tension, the melancholic mood, or the sense of anticipation that the work evokes. The choice of lighting, clothing, props, and time of day are all important elements. I choreograph each scene, making sure that my model's gestures, body language, and expressions all work together in such a way that they seem effortless.

> I believe that work needs to come from a place of truth. There was a time in the Double Life series when my model was pregnant, and I made photographs depicting one pregnant figure with one figure who was not pregnant. This work did not feel true to me because I had not experienced pregnancy. So, over the many years of making this project, those images have been edited out.

> I think that my photographs lie as documents yet tell greater truths as images. Because I did not document these two people at the same time and place, the images create a fiction. But because my photographs portray inner thoughts, vulnerabilities, and memories as tangible objects, an emotional truth is created. I tend to agree with Henry Peach Robinson, who said: "any dodge, trick, and conjuration of any kind is open to the photographer's use. A great deal can be done and very beautiful pictures made by a mixture of the real and artificial in a picture."

3. Is the idea of a body of work important to you? How does it function in relation to making a great individual photograph?

> The images that I make are particularly dependent on the body of work. For example, in Double Life, it is only when viewers have seen four to five of the images together that they then do a double take and go back to reexamine their thoughts about the first image. It is this reexamination that I am particularly interested in. It is pretty safe to say that my work would be interpreted differently if only one strong image was pulled out of the series. Something else to note is how the project

has progressed over time. I started Double Life in 2002, and its meaning has shifted, just as my ideas about the self, sexuality, relationships, and the body have evolved.

The photographs in my most recent body of work entitled Pictures for Charis, function in a similar way. While images are strong individually, the experience of reading the accompanying text is integral to shaping the overall meaning.

4. Do you have what you might call a "photographic style"?

Perhaps with the Double Life work, yes. I have had many people come up to me and say, "Hey, my student made some Kelli Connell images," referring to the fact that their student doubled themselves in an image. I know that my work is often used to teach compositing with Photoshop. Many people may associate seeing one subject doubled in the frame as something particular to Double Life, yet this way of working is not particularly new. Photographers have been making composites since the first years of photography. Oscar Rejlander made several composites, including *Two Ways of Life* in 1857, which was a combination print of thirty-two negatives. Each model posed separately for this scene, and the photograph itself took more than six weeks to make. Henry Peach Robinson as well as other Pictorialists made constructions. More contemporary examples include the collages of Claude Cahun and the digital composites of Anthony Goicolea.

5. Where would you say your style falls on a continuum between completely intuitive and intellectually formulated?

For me, it's a balance between these two approaches. In Double Life, the system for making the images has been figured out. I use the same camera (a Pentax 67), the same film (Kodak Portra), and one of two lenses. Each time we make work, I have a loose idea about the scene we are creating together. I may be interested in a particular location, such as the lakefront, the interior of a dive bar, or someone's bedroom. I may want to create an image that is atmospheric, an image that is practically black with only a few rays of light illuminating the scene. Or I may choose a particular action or emotion that will be used to decide the other elements in the frame. Most of the time I have an emotional tone in mind as I direct Kiba. But there is also a lot of intuition at play. Sometimes noticing a change in light can inspire a photograph in a new location. Or sometimes Kiba will move her body in a particular way that gives me a totally different idea. I work intuitively when it comes to the actual shooting of the images, but the original parameters help me find a good starting point.

6. Assuming you now shoot in what you would consider your natural voice, have you ever wished your voice was different?

No.

7. How do you know when a body of work is finished?

This has always been a challenge for me! I don't know if it's because I'm an Aries, but I have always enjoyed starting projects and had a hard time finishing things. This has manifest itself not just in my art practice but in other things that I take on.

For a while I felt pressure, whether self-imposed or otherwise, to complete Double Life. But I kept having ideas, and Kiba and I still enjoyed working together. Ending a body of work prematurely because of the pressures in the art world seems arbitrary to me. I feel that this work could continue for decades.

Pictures for Charis will definitely be a stand-alone body of work. The project is inspired by the time that Edward Weston and Charis Wilson were together from 1934 to 1945. My partner Betsy and I set out to California to explore the places where they lived and made work together, including stops from their Guggenheim travels, as well as places where they lived before and after that time, tracing their relationship from its start to their separation. Since the project is time-based, it has a natural end.

8. Have you ever had a body of work that was created in the editing process?

For Double Life, I initially work in a nonlinear way, creating single photographs that I have in mind, and it is through the editing process, whether for a book or an exhibition, that the edit solidifies itself. This can change each time that the work is exhibited, but because of the long-term nature of this project, the edit usually presents itself using a linear timeline as a guide. I think most photographic bodies of work are made in the editing process, and this can be exhilarating or excruciating.

9. Do you associate your work with a particular genre of photography? If yes, how would you define that genre?

No. This may go back to me not liking things to fit in boxes, but it has been interesting to see that my work can be framed in many different ways. The images in Double Life have been considered within many contexts, ranging from conversations about digital manipulation to portraiture and photographer-to-sitter relationships to explorations of self and queer identity. The variety of contexts in which the work has been shown opens the work to even wider interpretations. Much in the way that these images deny the assumption of static roles, or the possibility of a singular identity, the focus of the work itself constantly shifts from the technical to the conceptual, from the formal to the cinematic, and from the narrative to the sociopolitical, all depending on its viewing context.

10. Do you ever revisit a series that has already been exhibited or published to shoot more and add to it?

See above.

11. Do you ever revisit a series that has already been exhibited or published and *reedit* it?

See above.

12. Do you create with presentation in mind, be that a gallery show or a book?

I feel that presentation is an essential element in all of my work. With Double Life I always envisioned large-scale photographs to suggest the narrative or film-like quality. Pictures for Charis is being made with the book form in mind, loosely inspired by *California and the West* [1940], which was coauthored by Weston and Wilson and included twelve chapters written by Wilson with suites of images by Weston. ❍

Lois Conner

First camera:
My father gave me a 6-by-6 Yashica when I was nine. Though I didn't really understand the relationship between f-stops and shutter speeds until I was a teenager, I kept the f-stop at 8 and the speed at 125, so in bright sun my negatives looked pretty good.

First meaningful photobook:
American Photographs (1938) by Walker Evans

Lois Conner (born in New York, 1951) is a recipient of a Guggenheim Fellowship, New York State Council of the Arts Fellowship, and National Endowment for the Arts Fellowship, among other awards. Her books include *Life in a Box* (2010), *Lotus Leaves* (2018), and *Beijing: Contemporary and Imperial* (2014). She has held teaching positions over the course of three decades at such institutions as Yale University School of Art, Princeton University, and Sarah Lawrence College. Conner received her BFA in photography from Pratt Institute (1975) and MFA in photography from Yale University School of Art (1981). She lives in New York.

First meaningful exhibition:
My mentor and painting teacher took me to see the Walker Evans show at MoMA in the spring of 1971. I can still feel my young self being taken in by the photographs and the way they were drawn.

That summer I saw the Warhol exhibition at the Whitney, which also really changed the way I see and think about art.

1. What comes first for you: the idea for a project, or individual photographs that suggest a concept?

> Sometimes a few photographs from another body of work suggest the way forward. With my long-term China project, representations of the Chinese landscape began to appear in photographs that I was making in Europe with the 8-by-10 camera: in particular, in the Aosta Valley in Italy and the area around Pont de l'Abîme in France. In 1984, I applied for a Guggenheim Fellowship to write about Guilin and the karst formations along the Li River in China. This landscape was introduced to me in a class on Ming dynasty painting at Yale with Richard Barnhart. The long form of the hand scroll, which cordoned off an elongated, narrow sliver of the world, inspired me to change the form of my pictures. In 1982, I put aside the more classical 8-by-10 and began to use a 7-by-17 banquet camera. In Louisiana, where I taught in 1983, I photographed the flat languid landscape along the Mississippi River Delta, its long horizon echoing the physicality of the paintings that I had studied with Barnhart. During my first year in China, my idea about what the project was changed dramatically.

2. What are the key elements that must be present for you when you are creating a body of work? (Social commentary, strong form, personal connection, photographic reference...)

> The elements that must be present for me are historical, cultural, and personal connections to the landscape. The idea of "landscape as culture" is critical. Photographic references, form, and social commentary are essential but not primary.

3. Is the idea of a body of work important to you? How does it function in relation to making a great individual photograph?

> The body of work is what drives me forward. It's impossible to know when and where that "great individual photograph" is going to be. It must be part of a larger body of work, or it won't happen. But there are exceptions, such as the pictures of the ladder in Hangzhou from 1984, the Le Shan Buddha from 1986, and Tiananmen Square from 1998. In each of these instances, looking through the ground glass at these images gave me a sense of clarity, a reaffirmation of purpose. In China it's impossible to develop my film, so during the months I am there I have to rely on my memory of the ground glass image and my notes to

give myself confidence to continue. The first time I was in China it was nine months before I could see anything.

4. Do you have what you might call a "photographic style"?

If I were to describe my photographic style, I would say that the panorama informs my narrative.

5. Where would you say your style falls on a continuum between completely intuitive and intellectually formulated?

It would be in between the two. I like to think that it is completely intuitive, but there is always the construction of the idea that drives you to the place and allows you to begin.

6. Assuming you now shoot in what you would consider your natural voice, have you ever wished your voice was different?

I don't wish my voice was different, but I hope that it continues to develop and that I don't rely too much on what is expected of me.

In 1983 I made a group of ten pictures of Central Park in New York, then I took those same ten sheets and photographed a boatyard in Mandeville, Louisiana. In this double exposure, boats are nestled in the trees, but they make sense. And the surrealism that should have prevailed is subverted by the structure inherent in both layers. I often thought of these pictures and the accidental double exposures that continued throughout my work with the view camera, but I wasn't sure how to use them more fully to describe a landscape.

In 2010 and 2011, living for months as an artist-in-residence with Sol LeWitt's fresco paintings and drawings in Praiano, Italy, made me reconsider particular details in the landscape—jet trails, webs, nests, fences, stones, water drops, roads, walls, walkways, tiling, and mesh—as part of an organizing system that could be imposed on the landscape. His grids of line and sweeps of controlled color powerfully mesmerize, impose, suggest, and reverberate. So I began this new work by comparing the scale of LeWitt's paintings with small objects, then the landscape, through multiple exposures. And I worked in color. The photographs were made in many locations throughout Campania and begun at my "studio." His house, his paintings, the surrounding mountains, and the powerful, unrelenting Tyrrhenian Sea were a constant inspiration.

I drove and I walked around Campania, obsessed, in particular, by Pompeii, Vico Equense, Naples, Ravello, and Amalfi. I divided my time between these places, spending the mornings on my balcony studio and the afternoons in the landscape. Often the land offered up its own naturally doubled self (as in the olive groves), or perhaps my eyes were opened by the experience of the place and the power of the art, both the ancient and the modern.

7. How do you know when a body of work is finished?

Sometimes you know, sometimes not. When I was working on my portraits of pregnant women, it was an intensely focused time, and then it suddenly ended. Perhaps the connections to new subjects faded or I was distracted by new work. But that project was also one of the most difficult. As it ended and I had an exhibition, I was overwhelmed by the support of the women I had photographed, as so many of them came to the opening, which was on the night of a blinding snowstorm, stepping over the drifts and shielding their newborns to be with me.

8. Have you ever had a body of work that was created in the editing process?

When you make a book, you are re-creating the body of work through the editing and sequencing process. It's very different from an exhibition, because it is complete once it is published. With all my books and catalogues, I've had to think of my work in a different way than I did with the individual pictures or the body of work in its entirety. It's a good way to pause and rethink the work. Often when I finish a book, I long to continue the project, as I see what I missed, or what could make it more complete. With my office project Life in a Box [2010], there was an inexpensive catalogue for the show in Hong Kong that pulled all the work together, along with the essay, into a form that made me want to continue working.

9. Do you associate your work with a particular genre of photography? If yes, how would you define that genre?

I associate my work with the documentary style as in the work of Walker Evans (American Photographs, 1938) and Eugène Atget.

10. Do you ever revisit a series that has already been exhibited or published to shoot more and add to it?

> With my Navajo portraits, I worked intensely for almost a decade, driving cross-country every summer to work. Then, there were long pauses while I was working on other projects. I work differently now than I did in the 1990s, and much has changed out on the reservation. People don't gather in the same way in public places where I feel I could approach them without invading their space. So I've changed formats in response to these changes. Currently, most of the work I do there is in color, using the 8 by 10. Though I am still making portraits, I made a series of double exposures in response to invisible monuments in their history. Layering specific images through double and triple exposures extended the narrative in another way and allowed me to picture part of these histories. The Rez is a project that I will continue indefinitely.

11. Do you ever revisit a series that has already been exhibited or published and *reedit* it?

> With the China work (which has gone on for thirty-four years now), there are so many different aspects to the work. I would like to make exhibitions and books of some of these individual projects. The two that are currently under consideration for publication and exhibition are the portraits and the lotus abstractions. I continue to revisit both of these series, and others.

12. Do you create with presentation in mind, be that a gallery show or a book?

> In the beginning of a project, sometimes I am all over the place, so I'm unsure of the form of the pictures (yet plowing ahead anyway). This is evident in a project I am currently working on, portraits of people with guns. I started it in 2013, inspired by Civil War portraits of young men going off to war.
>
> I've circled around this subject for years. It seems, given the current political climate, that it may either be the best or the worst time to create this work. The first portraits were of my family. My sister and her daughter are champion shooters. They use muzzleloader guns, invented in 1610 in France, to shoot at targets. My brother and father were both hunters, and my father made and shot flintlock muzzleloaders. In the first pictures, a screen separated the person from the landscape, mimicking the look of the nineteenth-century studios where many

young soldiers had their portraits made. I also have a landscape painting (painted by a friend, after one of my photographs) that I use as a studio backdrop, and I'm in the process of painting a second one myself (as I trained to be a painter very early on). So far, there are 8-by-10 color portraits and solarized black-and-white ones. It's my attempt to visually isolate the subjects yet have the landscape be an essential part of the picture. I photograph people I know, friends of friends, and go to gun clubs with careful introductions. These portraits may never be in an exhibition or a book. But it's a critical project for me. ◑

Matthew Connors

First camera:
Minolta X-700

First meaningful photobook:
Diane Arbus: An Aperture Monograph (1972)

Matthew Connors (born in Port Washington, New York, 1976) lives and works in New York. His first book, *Fire in Cairo* (2015), was awarded the 2016 International Center of Photography Infinity Award for Artist's Book. Connors received his BA in English literature from the University of Chicago in 1998, and his MFA in photography from Yale University School of Art in 2004. Since 2004, he has been a professor in the photography department at the Massachusetts College of Art and Design, Boston.

First meaningful exhibition:
Motion and Document, Sequence and Time: Eadweard Muybridge and Contemporary American Photography, International Center of Photography, 1992

1. What comes first for you: the idea for a project, or individual photographs that suggest a concept?

> My projects tend to emerge out of a relationship between the two. That isn't to say images and ideas always carry equal weight at the outset. A body of work can propagate more directly from one, but they always redirect each other, usually to the point where I find it difficult to remember which came first. I like to believe that even my most intuitive and casually made photographs are conduits to my subconscious ideas. They are the result of a complicated meshwork of concepts, instincts, and observations that have been brewing inside me my whole life.

> When Flannery O'Connor began short stories, she didn't always know where they would lead. She wrote that after the bible salesman unexpectedly appeared halfway into "Good Country People," she didn't know he was going to steal Hulga's wooden leg until ten or twelve lines before he did. But when she found out it was going to happen, she said she realized it was inevitable. I've always felt a kinship with this way of thinking. I typically start with broad frameworks that allow me to follow unexpected threads and make discoveries en route.

2. What are the key elements that must be present for you when you are creating a body of work? (Social commentary, strong form, personal connection, photographic reference…)

> First, I'd say I have to be compelled by the subject and location. It is also important for me to have some sense that photographing them will bring me closer to an understanding I don't already have. This has recently led me to haunt the periphery of revolutionary activity in Cairo, glimpse the mechanisms of totalitarianism in North Korea, embed myself in the Occupy movement in New York, chart the legacy of revolutionary monuments in Cuba, and track paroxysms of protest in the wake of the 2016 United States presidential election.

> Good pictures can hit us with intellectual, emotional, and palpably somatic resonances that force us to call into question fundamental assumptions about our perceptions. Strong form can lead to this, but it can just as easily deliver received notions when it is deployed in a predictable manner. For me, the goal is for projects to be fluent in the medium's language and to leverage this to address problematic power relationships in the world.

3. Is the idea of a body of work important to you? How does it function in relation to making a great individual photograph?

> Photographs somehow feel unfinished if they are not part of a completed project. In fact, I'm haunted by particular images that I haven't been able to connect firmly to others yet. I've spent most of my life so far dedicated to creating thick descriptions of the world that coalesce around photographs in relationship to each another. Individual pictures can have potency, but I have always found carefully considered constellations of images—in books and on walls—to have the greatest potential for working out the issues most urgent to me.

4. Do you have what you might call a "photographic style"?

> I have projects that have their own internal stylistic coherence, elements of which can seep into other projects. But I have not pursued an overarching, signature style in my work. I'm skeptical of some of the motivations for that approach, and I think I would find it too limiting.

5. Where would you say your style falls on a continuum between completely intuitive and intellectually formulated?

> Somewhere in the middle. Where exactly depends on that particular body of work and at what stage of development it is in. While photographing I try to tap into whatever reservoirs of intuition I have. But I'm usually operating toward the other end of the continuum when I make decisions about which contexts to approach, what shape the engagement should take, and which tools to bring to the situation. As a body of work progresses and important motifs emerge, I become more preoccupied with the relationships between the pictures. It pushes me while photographing to make more conscious decisions about how new pictures can relate to existing ones.

> But I have to say, I've never fully trusted the dichotomy between intellect and intuition. These supposedly different ways of working completely overlap in my mind. Our intuitions are ways of very quickly bringing to bear a set of intellectual formulations we've developed about the world. They are constantly gestating in response to the culture we consume and the experiences we have. How my intuition inflects a picture at any given moment may be as influenced by my relationship with my father as by a puddle I stepped in the week prior. Paul Graham once called

a photographer's intuition their "liquid intelligence." That has always stayed with me.

6. Assuming you now shoot in what you would consider your natural voice, have you ever wished your voice was different?

I'd say I shoot with multiple voices and am not sure which ones I would consider natural. It's helpful for me to think of these voices as a collection of narrators, akin to those a novelist might employ over the span of her career. Some closely mirror my perspective. Others have the guise of omniscience. Some others are deeply flawed or unreliable.

There are projects that I consider to have a single, consistent voice, and others that are propelled by the tension between multiple narrators as in William Faulkner's *The Sound and the Fury*. I also like when a voice from one project resurfaces in another, as the way of describing a protester in *Fire in Cairo* [2015] echoes that of *General Assembly* [2013]. I'm always trying to modify my voices, and I expect several new ones will emerge in future projects.

7. How do you know when a body of work is finished?

I usually don't realize something is finished until long after it is done. Those who know me well say I tend to exhaust all options before finishing a body of work. Calling something complete can be the most difficult part of the process for me, and I have the tendency to forestall it until I'm ready to disengage from the material. These days I find producing a book to be the best way to achieve some sense of closure.

8. Have you ever had a body of work that was created in the editing process?

To some degree all bodies of work are made in the editing process. Even photographers with the most prescriptive practices discard images that don't work and bring together the ones that do. Some place more emphasis on it than others. For me, editing has become an increasingly important moment for a project to take shape. Over the past decade I've been transitioning from a slow photographer and fast editor to a fast photographer and slow editor. I attribute some of this to the technological gestations we've been experiencing, notably the replacement of film with sensors. But primarily I attribute it to realizing the deep potential in sustaining tensions between pictures. It can be one of the most difficult things to achieve though.

I'm at a point where I'm starting to reassess a fairly big archive of my images. I know there are a few bodies of work that can be coaxed out of it. But it is difficult to be disciplined about this with the knowledge that I have already spent some of the best years of my life in darkened rooms with backlit monitors, and there are still so many other pictures to make.

9. Do you associate your work with a particular genre of photography? If yes, how would you define that genre?

Multiple genres appear in my work so I don't think about it in relation to a particular one, but I am often thinking about how I can tamper with genre conventions in unexpected ways. Most of my work can be characterized as an engagement with the actual—often in specific currents of history—which I translate through a set of subjective visual interests. My hope is the result will reveal something about the complex of social, political, and cultural forces that shape our notions of reality. The pictures rely on some currency of truth, but one that has the potential of being counterfeit. The genre of literature I think this comes closest to is historical fiction.

10. Do you ever revisit a series that has already been exhibited or published to shoot more and add to it?

Yes, I will do that if a project is not finished when pictures from it are exhibited. But after I consider a project complete—mostly when I've finalized the form of the book—I almost never shoot more. If I do, it is not to fill a gap, but out of some personal curiosity or belief that it could be a starting point for something different.

11. Do you ever revisit a series that has already been exhibited or published and *reedit* it?

Strangely, I've had that experience with individual photographs. For years I worked on a project that involved a great deal of postproduction and compositing. After these pictures were first exhibited I realized I wanted to change some of them by digitally substituting some of their compositional elements. It was profound and terrifying to realize my photographs could be infinitely mutable even after they have been deployed in the world. But this was nearly fifteen years ago, when we were all still getting used to these ideas.

12. Do you create with presentation in mind, be that a gallery show or a book?

I usually don't. Scale, layout, sequence, and installation decisions don't tend to enter the scene until a body of work begins to take shape. However, I would say that over the years my imagination has become more calibrated to how pictures can be read on pages than how they are experienced on walls. This has had an impact on the way I see photographs before I take them. ◑

Siân Davey

First camera:
Mamiya 7

First meaningful photobook:
The River: Winter (2012)
by Jem Southam

Siân Davey (born in Brighton, UK, 1964) was a psychotherapist in private practice for fifteen years before earning an MA and MFA in photography in 2014 and 2016 from the University of Plymouth, UK. She has published two books to date: *Martha* (2018) and *Looking for Alice* (2015), for which she received the Royal Photographic Society Hood Medal Award. She lives in Devon, UK.

First meaningful exhibition:
Louise Bourgeois retrospective at the Tate Modern, London, in 2008. I was so profoundly moved by Bourgeois's unbridled compulsion to make work from her own history that, afterward, I sat on the steps outside the gallery and decided I was going to start a creative practice. A year or so later I chose photography as my medium.

Personal fact:
My mother was relocating, and together we packed up all her possessions (she was a hoarder) and off they went into storage. Just a few weeks later she died unexpectedly, and to this day I have no idea what happened to her possessions, but the lesson was profound. I don't feel any need to attach myself to material things apart from what my children or my friends create.

1. What comes first for you: the idea for a project, or individual photographs that suggest a concept?

> My first series [published in 2015] was about my youngest daughter, Alice, who was born with Down's syndrome. It was ignited by feelings of anger at how I felt others perceived her. I felt a need to articulate and disseminate these feelings. In that sense, the concept preempted the work.
>
> My following body of work, Martha [published in book form in 2018], was inspired by a photograph I had already taken of my eldest daughter. The strength of Martha's gaze caught hold of me and invited me into her world. It was unnerving to begin the Martha series with no concept, but letting myself go into the process of "not knowing" was liberating. I had to trust that the unconscious and conscious material of her life—and our relationship—would be revealed over time.
>
> The series I am currently working on, about my youngest son, Joseph, was inspired by an August Sander picture I saw in a gallery in Paris. I had photographed Joseph extensively two years before but didn't feel confident the project was working. Seeing the Sander print felt like a transmission—in that moment I knew exactly what I needed to do. I have always worked in medium format (6-by-7) but decided, like Sander, to work in large format (8-by-10). Working this way strips everything down. All I am left with is myself, Joseph, and our shared histories revealing themselves in that single moment. Furthermore, all my series are essentially collaborations; they are also consensual. Joseph, being fourteen years old, doesn't want his mother to be alongside him all of his life, so to work in a confined space makes the process possible for him.

2. What are the key elements that must be present for you when you are creating a body of work? (Social commentary, strong form, personal connection, photographic reference...)

> A larger body of work allows a story to reveal itself over time. There are so many layers and meanings to life. Working over an extended period allows this material to be revealed. But it only does so when it's ready to show itself. Such is the magic of the photographic journey.

3. Is the idea of a body of work important to you? How does it function in relation to making a great individual photograph?

> Both are equally relevant. An individual photograph can be as powerful as an entire body of work—it entirely depends on the overarching concept and the intention of the author.

4. Do you have what you might call a "photographic style"?

> I identify more with the idea of a voice than a photographic style. Rather than reference myself outside, I look inward, communicating from my own DNA. Photography is everywhere, therefore we are vulnerable to losing the ability to decipher our own unique voice. With that in mind, I often advise students to confine their research to galleries until they feel they have a strong enough sense of who they are and what they need to say.

5. Where would you say your style falls on a continuum between completely intuitive and intellectually formulated?

> It's fluid. As I work, I move between my intellectual and intuitive self. It's about knowing we can make a choice, and learning to do that. It's a dance between them both.

> The thinking mind is often needed to inform a moment or help us through a process of inquiry. But equally, the thinking mind can stop us from seeing and responding to the unconscious material out there. It can close down the adventure and infinite possibilities of the unknown. Working intuitively takes us into the territory of surrender. When we relinquish the "self" there is the potential to feel the interconnectedness between everything—you, me, my history, and yours. Ultimately it all comes down to presence, being awake and staying in contact with the world around you.

6. Assuming you now shoot in what you would consider your natural voice, have you ever wished your voice was different?

> No, because that would be a rejection of self.

> I discovered photography in my mid-forties and have used it to carry out an in-depth personal inquiry. Because I came to the work a bit later

in life, I maybe had a stronger sense of self, and that enabled my natural voice to flow from the beginning.

7. How do you know when a body of work is finished?

I know when a body of work is finished when the charge drops, and the thing that pulled you along is no longer there. You can feel yourself lose your connection to the narrative. At this point, the story has been told and is now in danger of repeating itself. It's about knowing when that time has come and having the courage to let it go.

8. Have you ever had a body of work that was created in the editing process?

No, I haven't. But I love the editing process, because it always reveals elements of the work that weren't apparent to me during the shoot. It allows me to recognize the unconscious material that is at play during the capturing process.

9. Do you associate your work with a particular genre of photography? If yes, how would you define that genre?

I'm interested in portraiture, people, and social narratives, but I don't identify with any genre. My work is perhaps rooted in documentary photography, but my practice is always evolving—as I am. And my approach to life in general is to challenge perceptions.

Labels are reductive. To say "I am this" or "You are that" means we fall into the trap of being positional and holding our identity in that label. It doesn't accommodate or allow for the process of inevitable change.

10. Do you ever revisit a series that has already been exhibited or published to shoot more and add to it?

I have two distinct ways of working. The work with my children requires a beginning and an end and a particular process of inquiry. It demands so much of me both intimately and intellectually, so only when I've answered the questions I let go. But I always have another series on the go, which I call The River. The project gives me the freedom to photograph people I meet in the landscape, as I take a walk with my camera or meet people at a summer festival, for example. It's important to me that this work is free from emotional attachments. It is spacious. Ultimately, it is my time-out.

11. Do you ever revisit a series that has already been exhibited or published and *reedit* it?

>I am sure I will in the future, but I don't think I've gotten to that stage yet. My passion is currently in new work.

12. Do you create with presentation in mind, be that a gallery show or a book?

>Making a book of my first project, Looking for Alice [2015], felt like an inevitability. The photobook is the perfect form for me because, through sequencing, it allows us to tell the story exactly as it should be told. And, a photobook also makes the work accessible to an audience beyond the photographic community. That said, a curated exhibition can allow the work to breathe again—within that space, we can find other ways of communicating the story. ◑

Davey

"I'm very interested in how pictures shift and change meaning over time. Musicians will revisit and revise their work over time and with each performance— visual artists are no different."

Doug DuBois

First camera:
An Agfa Rangefinder I discovered in a hall closet when I was twelve or thirteen. My father had bought it when he was in the navy.

First meaningful photobook:
Man and Machine (1971) by Henri Cartier-Bresson. The book was commissioned by IBM. My best friend and I would look at the book for hours, making up stories to go with the pictures.

Doug DuBois (born in Dearborn, Michigan, 1960) has received fellowships from the Guggenheim Foundation, MacDowell Colony, and National Endowment for the Arts. His monographs are *All the Days and Nights* (Aperture, 2009) and *My Last Day at Seventeen* (with graphic component by Patrick Lynch; Aperture, 2015). DuBois received a BA in film and photography from Hampshire College in 1983 and an MFA in photography from the San Francisco Art Institute in 1988. He is an associate professor at Syracuse University.

First meaningful exhibition:
I'll never forget seeing the first US iteration of Gerhard Richter's *Atlas* at the Dia Art Foundation in Chelsea in 1996. The exhibition taught me more about the work of art and photography than anything I've seen before or since.

Personal fact:
My first editorial assignment ever came from the *Telegraph Magazine* in London in 1994. They asked me to photograph John Wayne Bobbitt, who was touring strip clubs to promote his video, *John Wayne Bobbitt Uncut*. If you don't know who he is, just do a quick search on the web. If you do, enough said.

1. What comes first for you: the idea for a project, or individual photographs that suggest a concept?

> Can I say both? For me, it's kind of a chicken/egg, words/music thing, or maybe just a faulty memory about how a particular body of work began. I certainly photographed my family with intent [*All the Days and Nights*, 2009], but it took making a critical number of photographs and a significant amount of time—decades, really—to understand how the images could work together. The photographs were smarter than I was at the time of their making, and I had to grow into the work.
>
> In Ireland, it all seemed to happen at once [*My Last Day at Seventeen*, 2015]. The opportunity to photograph Irish youth and the notion (however inarticulate) that this idea might be sustainable over time occurred in one night of meeting people and making pictures. While that may sound easy, that evening came after two weeks of making terrible photographs of no consequence.
>
> The work precedes the idea, and the idea initiates the work. I don't think one necessarily comes before the other—it's a conversation.

2. What are the key elements that must be present for you when you are creating a body of work? (Social commentary, strong form, personal connection, photographic reference...)

> A personal/political/social connection—it's hard to separate meanings and motivations. There's a political and social dimension to everything, especially creative decisions, but the motivation—the thing that drives you to keep making the work, especially when it's rough and unformed, that's a very personal commitment. If I can't place or imagine myself in the work, it generally doesn't amount to much. *How* I manage to locate myself—as an insider, outsider, voyeur, participant, director, advocate, whatever—necessarily requires negotiation, trust, and an entanglement in the politics of each.
>
> The personal motivates me to make the work, and the political teaches me (and by extension, the viewer or reader) about my place in the world and more or less frames the meaning for the work.
>
> Here's a small example: More than fifteen years ago, I was making, as an exercise more than anything else, extended series of portraits constrained by a specific place, a time of day, a street corner, etc.

One project involved going to the New York State Fair [in Syracuse] to make portraits on the midway. I noticed people carrying all sorts of absurd prizes from the carnival games and thought I could make something out of a person's bearing and their choice of prize. But with no clear explanation about what I was doing and why, nearly everyone turned me down. After a few hours of work and precious few portraits, I simply asked a teenage boy carrying a large Bubbles, the Powerpuff Girl, "Did you win that? I'm doing a project about winners, can I take your picture?" He puffed up his chest a bit and said, "Yes." Being a winner is fundamental to American identity and is, of course, what motivates people to spend money on the midway. Once I tapped into that—once I found a political frame for my personal and rather inchoate portrait series—I rarely got turned down for a photograph.

3. Is the idea of a body of work important to you? How does it function in relation to making a great individual photograph?

Bettina Lockemann, a very smart photographer and scholar from Germany, wrote a quite accessible essay with the intimidating title "A Phenomenological Approach to the Photobook." She borrows and expands upon Allan Sekula's distinction between a photographic series, where images relate to each other in terms of themes and variations, but do not demand a specific order or number of images to articulate the idea of the work, and a sequence, which specifies an order and a number of images to fully engage the idea(s) of the work.

While I've worked both ways, I'm most drawn to the demands of sequential editing and tend to build up a body of work by keeping a loose sense of narrative in mind. But the goal remains for each image to conjure up a whole world on its own, and despite my interest in putting photographs together, I can only work on one image at a time.

Whether a series or a sequence, the accretion of photographs can offer more than a single image. Ten water towers, presented in a grid, offer opportunities for formal, taxonomic, and archival considerations that a single image cannot. Similarly, six carefully sequenced photographs of a woman eating chicken at a bus stop present to the imagination a world, a time of day and in history, a life and a place (geographic and economic), smells, textures, and sounds that a single image cannot quite muster.

But then, there's the photograph of three masked children on a stoop in New York during Halloween circa 1940—a small miracle that I'll never tire of seeing and thinking about.

4. Do you have what you might call a "photographic style"?

If people can recognize your work, I guess that means you have a style, but it's a term I've never felt comfortable with and rarely use. I can't frame my work with a *high*-concept description of style—maybe that's snobbish or simply a coy avoidance of the question—but I think I'll leave it there.

5. Where would you say your style falls on a continuum between completely intuitive and intellectually formulated?

If we can substitute artistic process for style, I'd say somewhere in the middle: always longing for better intuition and working hard toward making my work smarter.

6. Assuming you now shoot in what you would consider your natural voice, have you ever wished your voice was different?

Voice is a good way to talk about an artist's point of view. I don't know if I'd consider my artist/authorial voice natural, I think it's always affected in one way or another, but there are certainly ways of seeing and telling that feel more comfortable and authentic. Am I envious of other artists' voices? Absolutely. Do I try out other approaches to making a photograph? All the time. More often than not the results are simply derivative, but the effort is hardly wasted: each attempt shifts my perspective and shapes my way of working in small and large ways.

7. How do you know when a body of work is finished?

Deadlines help and are often critical to preventing something from getting overthought and overworked. I've been lucky to have some good book editors who, more than once, kept me from ruining a good idea.

Repetition is another sign—but it's tricky. Going back again and again to a certain subject or making variations is an important discipline. The bad repetition, the kind that doesn't add up to anything and becomes a dead end or a compulsive gesture—that's a sign that you are done with a project.

Then there's always the chance that the people you are working with simply declare, "I've had enough." Usually, I figure that out before someone has to tell me—but not always.

8. Have you ever had a body of work that was created in the editing process?

Pretty much everything I do is made in the editing process—it's a necessary skill that's not easily acquired—you have to work at it and/or work with someone who has experience. It begins with the initial cull—something that has become harder, I think, as the rate of image production accelerates—and ends with a process of distillation that gathers together the essential ideas, forms, colors, emotions, whatever is critical to the work.

There are a lot of techniques and frameworks to guide you through the process. Jim Goldberg helped me a great deal on my first book. He broke it down to a few simple steps: make piles of small prints, find a system that allows for quick changes and play, and most important, give yourself time and room for false starts and detours.

Editing can be an exhausting process, but it's as critical for a photographer as it is for filmmakers and writers. Some of the best guides for editing come from both: Michael Ondaatje's interviews with Walter Murch, *The Conversations: Walter Murch and the Art of Editing Film*; John McPhee's *Draft No. 4: On the Writing Process* (his daughter is the brilliant photographer, Laura McPhee), and Susan Bell's *The Artful Edit* (it has an insightful account of F. Scott Fitzgerald's working relationship with his editor Maxwell Perkins as well as a very useful anecdote about Bell's husband, Mitch Epstein, struggling with editing for an exhibition).

9. Do you associate your work with a particular genre of photography? If yes, how would you define that genre?

Documentary-esque? I can't invent images out of whole cloth, and there's nothing more terrifying than the blank white of a studio. I'm dependent, for better or worse, on an existing world and lived experience to create my images. The ethos of documentary—that embattled and embittered claim to truth, justice, and the American Way—is an important but never-ending argument that complicates the term and makes it difficult for me to use without qualification. It'd be disingenuous, however, to imply that my way of working sits outside of or in opposition to documentary practice. More often than not, I photograph with the visual rhetoric and conceits that are associated with documentary photography, but I don't follow the rules that disallow invention, direction, and a host of subjectivities guided by a collaborative (as opposed to an objective) striving for a truth. I think if you look at the world with clarity and pay attention to how and why the world could stare back at you, then documentary might be an adequate—but not necessary—term to use as a framework for your practice.

10. Do you ever revisit a series that has already been exhibited or published to shoot more and add to it?

Yes, of course. I'm very interested in how pictures shift and change meaning over time. Musicians will revisit and revise their work over time and with each performance—visual artists are no different.

My family photographs from *All the Days and Nights* have been shown in various iterations since the late 1980s. Over the years, the photographs became about ageing, loss, and time. In that sense, new photographs can add meaning and nuance to the work as time passes.

I'm unlikely, however, to revisit the photographs in *My Last Day at Seventeen* in any significant way. Not so much because I think the book is definitive, but because the photographs speak to a specific and fragile moment of youth that demands the suspension of time. I don't see the point of photographing Eirn, Kevin, or Roisin as they age—not because their lives aren't significant, but because youth can't hold out against age.

11. Do you ever revisit a series that has already been exhibited or published and *reedit* it?

Exhibitions, yes—publications, not yet.

12. Do you create with presentation in mind, be that a gallery show or a book?

When I began photographing my family again after a six- or seven-year break, my goal was to make a book. And while I didn't photograph to complete a specific sequence, several of the later photographs were directed and posed to refer to images made ten or twenty years earlier.

In Ireland, when someone asked me what I would do with the photographs, I promised they would be exhibited in the local arts center and maybe put into a book, but at the outset of the project, at least, I had no idea if either would happen. I was just trying to explain my presence in the community and answer the very legitimate question, "What are you going to do with the pictures?"

During my last summer in Ireland to photograph, I had already exhibited the work and had a maquette of the book. I made less than a handful of photographs of consequence. There's a difference between having a book in mind and one, however tentative, in hand. Once the body of work is nearly realized, things get very finicky—the work seems to push back and resist change. This is, of course, another indication that the work is nearly finished. ◑

DuBois

"The ubiquity of the photographic image that many perceive as photography's weakness is its strength. I am compelled by any pictures in the world that really slow me down."

John
Edmonds

First camera:
Digital point-and-shoot camera
(I don't remember the brand)

First meaningful photobook:
Philip-Lorca diCorcia's *Hustlers* (2013)

John Edmonds (born in Washington, DC, 1989) received his BFA
in photography from the Corcoran School of the Arts and Design
(2012) and his MFA in photography from Yale University School
of Art (2016). He was the recipient of the inaugural Capricious
Photo Award, which led to his debut monograph *Higher* (2018).
Edmonds lives and works in Brooklyn.

First meaningful exhibition:
30 Americans at the Corcoran Gallery
of Art, Washington, DC, in 2011

1. What comes first for you: the idea for a project, or individual photographs that suggest a concept?

> Often ideas come to me when I'm sitting with previous work and trying to find a thread that connects it to a newer set of pictures that I have been thinking of making. I like to find ways to build upon themes or concepts that were planted as seeds, but not fully fleshed out.
>
> All artists are different. What I have noticed, as an introvert, is that the work often comes from long periods of reading and researching, looking and sitting by myself. Once I feel like I have hit the ceiling with thinking, there needs to be some action. This does not necessarily mean photographing. It may mean going out to a party, an opening, a get-together of some sort. I am inspired by people, life, and conversation. This is usually where ideas are sparked and one conversation leads to another. It really happens in this electric way that shows how everything, in some shape or form, is connected. Being patient and self-aware and open to what the universe gives is central. Pictures inform other pictures, and projects inform other projects. It's not so linear, and more of a web.

2. What are the key elements that must be present for you when you are creating a body of work? (Social commentary, strong form, personal connection, photographic reference...)

> I have to have a sincere interest and connection to the content. This does not necessarily mean that it has to be personal, but I have to feel connected and have a sense of desire to go beyond the facade of the subject. I am not interested in pictures merely as documents or records of a person, place, or thing.
>
> I like to be able to see the formal beauty in things, so a level of control is necessary. Photographing people primarily allows for a little push and pull, just a little friction. Control is as important and necessary as lack of control, for something serendipitous to happen. This is true mainly in how I think of light. I use ambient light 98 percent of the time, so in a way, I am always following the light.

3. Is the idea of a body of work important to you? How does it function in relation to making a great individual photograph?

> I appreciate when an image has the power to stand on its own. An image that is able to do this is one that usually catches and holds my attention. In a body of work, an image should be able to add to what is happening thematically or conceptually. Context is great, but I feel it's most important to have the image speak directly to the viewer.

4. Do you have what you might call a "photographic style"?

> I consider myself a formalist. Style is always evolving and changing, as it should.

5. Where would you say your style falls on a continuum between completely intuitive and intellectually formulated?

> Somewhere in between. I like to be very considerate of all formal elements. However, intuition is central. It's about when it feels right, and that is a highly subjective thing.

6. Assuming you now shoot in what you would consider your natural voice, have you ever wished your voice was different?

> No. The key is nurturing your own talents and abilities. You cannot be someone you are not, and there is no reason in trying.

7. How do you know when a body of work is finished?

> The work is never "finished." I just continue the ideas in the following project, and I know when I am ready to move on. When something is published or exhibited, I consider it an iteration of the work. The goal is to see where the work can take you next.

8. Have you ever had a body of work that was created in the editing process?

> Editing is central. The work is made in the editing process.

9. Do you associate your work with a particular genre of photography? If yes, how would you define that genre?

> I think it's a bit dated to marry one's work only to a specific style or genre. I am interested in the art of the in-between, and I believe this is strongly achieved in photography. Photography as a moving currency is what makes it interesting—its ability to move from one context to another, such as journalism to fine art or print to online. Ultimately, I believe that the ubiquity of the photographic image that many perceive as photography's weakness is its strength. I am compelled by any pictures in the world that really slow me down.

10. Do you ever revisit a series that has already been exhibited or published to shoot more and add to it?

> Yes, more often than not, I like to add work into previous series. I may stop working on something, but that does not mean it cannot be revisited and reconsidered with fresh eyes and a deeper perspective.

11. Do you ever revisit a series that has already been exhibited or published and *reedit* it?

> I add images into a series but don't reedit.

12. Do you create with presentation in mind, be that a gallery show or a book?

> After making work for a while, you begin to understand how it may take form when installed. This does not mean that you have to restrict yourself to these confines, but it can help knowing how your work translates in exhibition form. I try to remain as open as possible, but I know myself. It's a balance. In short, I would say that I never make work considering how it will be installed or how it would look in a show. However, once I start considering how things are coming together, that does inform decisions. ◑

LaToya Ruby Frazier

First camera:
Nikon FM10

First meaningful photobook:
Half Past Autumn: A Retrospective
by Gordon Parks (1997)

LaToya Ruby Frazier (born in Braddock, Pennsylvania, 1982)
received a BFA in applied media arts from Edinboro University,
Pennsylvania, in 2004, and an MFA in art photography from
Syracuse University in 2007. Frazier is associate professor of
photography at the School of the Art Institute of Chicago and the
recipient of numerous awards, including a MacArthur Fellowship;
International Center of Photography Infinity Award; John Simon
Guggenheim Foundation Fellowship; and Gwendolyn Knight
and Jacob Lawrence Prize, Seattle Art Museum. Her publications
include *And From the Coaltips a Tree Will Rise* (2017) and *The
Notion of Family* (Aperture, 2014). Frazier is based in Chicago.

First meaningful exhibition:
Larry Clark at the International
Center of Photography in 2005

Personal fact:
I think that it is absurdly fitting that
because I have lupus, my skin is literally
photosensitive. I have become one with
my medium.

1. What comes first for you: the idea for a project, or individual photographs that suggest a concept?

   I truly believe that amateur photographers and professional photographers alike need to be guided by the work, to let the images lead to the next image, and to the next stage. It's a process. I allow a body of work to lead to the next body of work.

2. What are the key elements that must be present for you when you are creating a body of work? (Social commentary, strong form, personal connection, photographic reference...)

   As a teacher, I teach it all. The concept, the formal qualities, the technique and aesthetic. All of these elements have to reinforce the content and the subject. I ask: How does the work relate to the history of photography and the history of art? These are the top concerns. Following that, there's another set of categories: the personal, the political, the economic, the social. I teach students how to take up their own interests and to translate it into work. It's important to ask: are your intentions clear? It's up to the individual artist to decide how much emphasis to place on each particular layer.

3. Is the idea of a body of work important to you? How does it function in relation to making a great individual photograph?

   It's always about a body of work for me. I don't do "projects." A project assumes that there is a beginning and an end—a body of work is a commitment to a lifelong endeavor of investigation and learning.

4. Do you have what you might call a "photographic style"?

   I don't know that I would say I have a photographic style, but what's important is how the trajectory of an inquiry is sustained. In my case, I care about social documentary work in the twenty-first century and about how that speaks to the early twentieth century. I try to conscientiously bring those ideas into conversation with a conceptually informed approach to making art—one that talks about the politics of everyday life. I am interested in using photography to unpack questions about how the images were made, how they relate to the subject's life.

   I'm also always interested in creating various entry points. I think it's important to ask: Who is making the work, and for whom? Who controls that narrative, and how is that disseminated to the general public? How does it relate to institutions and to power? My style may change according to the need and to the situation at hand.

5. Where would you say your style falls on a continuum between completely intuitive and intellectually formulated?

In all of my work, my main concern is in making intellectual and conceptual inquiries. I can deploy several different styles in a single body of work. You need to know how to speak according to different aesthetic modes and visual languages; this leads to a more democratic way of expressing yourself through images. I'm not interested in just one aesthetic. I can use portraiture, landscapes—ultimately it's all social commentary to me. You need to be able to access and use all of these visual languages in order to give multiple entry points to different viewers and perspectives.

6. Assuming you now shoot in what you would consider your natural voice, have you ever wished your voice was different?

No. My voice is shaped in collaboration with the people I photograph, so it's continually adapting. There's no single fixed voice, and I would never want to be that static. I want to be flexible and responsive to the language of the people with whom I'm working.

7. How do you know when a body of work is finished?

It will never be finished. The meaning of an image is never fixed. It changes as history changes. We're all connected intergenerationally—we're connected to the images of the past and to the future. I'm thinking about time travel when I make my work—take, as an example, my work with my mother and my grandmother [The Notion of Family, 2014]. I'm suggesting we are one entity; we are all markers on a timeline that is cyclical. But even within that work, things change. Take the self-portrait Huxtables, Mom, and Me [2008]. I'm wearing a T-shirt that's worn, the ink is peeling off; the mirror behind me, in which a reflection of my mom can be seen, is dusty and scratched. The image already had meaning embedded in it because of what the Huxtables meant to American society—the first public image of a middle-class black family and the whole "Cosby effect" that I wanted to critique. Looking at it now, thanks to Bill Cosby's sex crimes, that image has acquired a whole new layer of meaning.

Frazier

8. Have you ever had a body of work that was created in the editing process?

I believe that you have to make the work and then allow it to speak to you. I don't think that one should self-censor or edit oneself aggressively while creating—there's a risk that you will self-impose limits on the work. Photography is about time, and you have to invest a lot of time before you realize what a body of work should be and how it should be edited. A body of work reveals itself over time.

9. Do you associate your work with a particular genre of photography? If yes, how would you define that genre?

My work is connected to two things: 1930s social documentary work and how it performed in relation to power structures of its time. I'm interested in the inherent hierarchy around how those images were made and how the aesthetics of that genre were informed by power relations. Where I depart from the 1930s-style is in my commitment to giving a voice to the subjects—this is a practice that is radically rooted in the personal and the political. I call it conceptual documentary art— equally influenced by 1960s and '70s work by people like Martha Rosler, Carrie Mae Weems, Allan Sekula, and other artists who talked about and made use of the politics of everyday life. My work is also intended for advocacy and efficacy—I am engaged in real political issues and real change. My images lead me to find ways to help the people I'm working with; I sell the work to give back to the communities I photograph. It goes beyond just taking pictures.

10. Do you ever revisit a series that has already been exhibited or published to shoot more and add to it?

Yes. That's what I do. We are constantly changing and rethinking our ideas. It's important to go back and to figure out how these things work.

11. Do you ever revisit a series that has already been exhibited or published and *reedit* it?

To paraphrase James Baldwin, nothing is fixed under the heavens. So, yes.

12. Do you create with presentation in mind, be that a gallery show or a book?

Once you find your voice and your vision, you should think about your audience and how best to engage with them. I'm always asking: How will this help an audience member understand what's happening here? How would a video instead of a still photograph work? Would a panel or public talk add to the audience's engagement with the material? I'm constantly thinking about multiple platforms and about how to better address my audience. My subject matter and content are already outside of the insular photo and art worlds—that's not who my work is for. I want the work to be as democratic as possible, and to make it work across as many platforms as possible, and to allow as many people to enter and engage with it as possible. My work is for everybody. ❍

Frazier

"It's fine to be influenced and work through those whose work changed your outlook. I certainly have, and I managed to come out the other side whole, and wholly myself."

Paul Graham

First camera:
Olympus OM-2, bought for me in
Hong Kong by a neighbor who was
a British Airways pilot

First meaningful photobook:
Public Relations (1977)
by Garry Winogrand

British photographer **Paul Graham** (born in Stafford, UK, 1956)
lives and works in New York. Over the past three decades, he
has produced thirteen distinct bodies of work and published a
dedicated monograph for nearly every series, including the twelve-
volume *a shimmer of possibility* (2007), which received the 2011
Paris Photo–Aperture Foundation PhotoBook Award for the most
important photography book published in the previous fifteen
years. Graham is the recipient of numerous other honors and
grants, including the Deutsche Börse Photography Prize and the
Hasselblad Foundation International Award. He has a degree and
honorary doctorate, but is self-taught in photography.

First meaningful exhibition:
Probably Van Gogh, in Paris

Personal fact:
At three years old, I burned my corneas
when I fell into a bag of very alkaline
cement powder. I spent three months
blind, wearing dark glasses and using a
stick, and then my corneas grew back
enough to begin to see. I remember the
utter joy of a pinhole of vision returning.

1. What comes first for you: the idea for a project, or individual photographs that suggest a concept?

> They go hand in glove. If you are a photographer who works with life, then you have to put yourself into the territory where that imagery and your thoughts might coalesce, because you need the vital lesson that first key image provides. Not the first image, but the first *key* image, the one that unlocks the door. The one you stumble over. It might surprise you by coming in from left field, taking things in a completely different direction, but that's the beauty of working with the world, with the moments that time hurls your way. It's a collaborative dance between the artist and life itself, so embrace the partnership. Often the world's complexity is far more interesting than your concepts. If you can have the humility to admit that, you'll do well.

2. What are the key elements that must be present for you when you are creating a body of work? (Social commentary, strong form, personal connection, photographic reference...)

> Different bodies of work emphasize different elements. One might be more socially critical, another more personal. Different approaches work, so there are no hard and fast rules, and don't let anyone tell you otherwise. Personally, I like it best when work is the perfect combination of speaking about life, while also illuminating something about the act of seeing itself. You come away from that and walk down the street, perceiving the world differently.

3. Is the idea of a body of work important to you? How does it function in relation to making a great individual photograph?

> Yes, of course a body of work is important, as the whole should be greater than the sum of its parts. Although there are times when people just want to make perfectly polished one-off pieces, and that is fine. Live and let live.

4. Do you have what you might call a "photographic style"?

> Please save me from the tragedy of a fixed "style"... No thank you!

5. Where would you say your style falls on a continuum between completely intuitive and intellectually formulated?

> See above. I tend to be a follower of what Garry Winogrand said (I paraphrase) about how "the world is far more interesting than any of my opinions concerning it." Compare something like Jeff Wall's photograph *In front of a nightclub* [2006] with what is found by Winogrand's finely tuned eye in *Public Relations* [1977], for example, and you see the vitality of that statement.

6. Assuming you now shoot in what you would consider your natural voice, have you ever wished your voice was different?

> There are certainly artists whose "voices" I've admired. But maybe some of them felt the same, so it all balances out. You clearly see some of Walker Evans's *American Photographs* [1938] voice in Robert Frank's *The Americans* [1958], then, in turn, you see Frank in early black-and-white William Eggleston. It's fine to be influenced and work through those whose work changed your outlook. I certainly have, and I managed to come out the other side whole, and wholly myself. Rock on, I say!

7. How do you know when a body of work is finished?

> When the question "Does this work?" is not keeping me awake anymore. At that point you have the answer to the thing that has been troubling you, so in a way it is, or will soon be, finished, and you can start to think ahead to the future.

8. Have you ever had a body of work that was created in the editing process?

> Yes, but then, photographers who deal with life are out there editing the world itself into photographs, so isn't every body of work made in the editing process? I'm not trying to be glib, I mean it: we edit the world, we find patterns in the entropy of life, we search for order in Brownian motion, so we have made the big, hard edit, and that is something to be proud of and remember when it comes to refining it even tighter.

9. Do you associate your work with a particular genre of photography? If yes, how would you define that genre?

> Not really. People tend to attach to my work a "documentary" label, but that's just silly. Is Eggleston documentary? Diane Arbus? Robert Adams? Thomas Struth? It's not helpful, so let's be smarter than just throwing that term around. Plus, we are definitely in a post-documentary era now, with still photography. It should also be pointed out that video has become the natural home for more classic "documentary" projects. It is far easier—every camera, every phone has a 4K video option now, the economic and technical barriers have completely evaporated. Very exciting, if that's your thing.

10. Do you ever revisit a series that has already been exhibited or published to shoot more and add to it?

> Nope. Move on. Grow. I might find a new way to install it in a show that looks back, but that is keeping things alive for me, as much as anything.

11. Do you ever revisit a series that has already been exhibited or published and *reedit* it?

> Nope. Never have. Life is too short.

12. Do you create with presentation in mind, be that a gallery show or a book?

> It used to be books, now it's more fifty-fifty. I love and enjoy the challenges of both. Books were what I educated myself with; they were how I "found" photography, and how it found me in a distant English city, so I embrace that fully. There is a dialogue among photographer-artists through books; it is more egalitarian than the art gallery system as there's no hierarchy—a great book is a great book—so it's very special. Galleries and museums can be wonderful moving spaces to see work in its ultimate form, with full-scale images in dialogue with each other, and in some ways with the world. So, I guess I'm saying: both matter. ◑

Katy Grannan

First camera:
Kodak Instamatic 124

First meaningful photobook:
The Americans (1958) by Robert Frank. I also remember that my grandparents had a copy of *The Family of Man* (edited by Edward Steichen, 1955), and even as a young kid I thought it was bullshit, or at least Pollyannaish and condescending. I appreciated far more the kinds of photographs that were unabashed, tough, and mysterious.

Katy Grannan (born in Arlington, Massachusetts, 1969) received a BA from the University of Pennsylvania in 1991, an MA from Harvard Medical School in 1993, and an MFA in photography from Yale University School of Art in 1999. Five monographs of her work have been published to date: *Model American* (Aperture, 2005), *The Westerns* (2007), *Boulevard* (2011), *The Nine* (2014), and *The Ninety-Nine* (2014). In 2015, Grannan released the feature film *The Nine*. She lives in Berkeley, California.

First meaningful exhibition:
Not really sure—but my grandparents always had issues of *Life* magazine, and I was obsessed with them, with their candor and harsh truths. I'd never seen anything like them.

1. What comes first for you: the idea for a project, or individual photographs that suggest a concept?

> Work flows from other work, ideas come from anywhere and at any time—and sometimes, not at all. I just keep working, keep living my life and trusting my curiosity. To be absolutely candid, though, a low-grade panic surfaces when I don't feel productive or inspired, and I have to talk myself down from the ledge and just keep showing up to work.

2. What are the key elements that must be present for you when you are creating a body of work? (Social commentary, strong form, personal connection, photographic reference...)

> I need to be engaged on a number of levels—visually, of course, and also intellectually, but the critical element is the one I can't name—it's a gut-level thing that grabs hold of me and sets in motion an irrational, unrelenting commitment to some unknown end. It's always a leap of faith.

3. Is the idea of a body of work important to you? How does it function in relation to making a great individual photograph?

> Sometimes a "body" of work is important in that it can be a way to orient myself and get specific—specificity allows me to go deeper, and it allows for nuance. But the true body of work is the sum total of a life's work. Projects are just chapters. Regardless, every photograph has to stand on its own.

4. Do you have what you might call a "photographic style"?

> I suppose I do, although I'm constantly challenging myself to try new ways of working. In the last few years I made a couple of films, and it was thrilling to feel like a beginner again. It dramatically changed the way I see, and it's affected my photography practice for sure. Still, I often make a mountain of work in the beginning stages and then slowly remove most of it, until it almost seems silly that it took me so long to get to a place that was in front of me the whole time. Initially, I cast a wide net and trust my way forward, but ultimately I toss everything that feels like I'm trying too hard or spreading myself thin. The appearance of complexity doesn't mean it's complex.

5. Where would you say your style falls on a continuum between completely intuitive and intellectually formulated?

It's not one or the other. I'm intuitive for sure, but it's not like I'm floating in the ether without a tethered thought in mind. The brain and the heart and the gut work in tandem—there is no hierarchy of value for me. I trust my instincts, and as goofy and unintellectual as it sounds, I lead with my heart. Creative work in any medium that's based on an "intellectually formulated construct" sounds dead on arrival to me. That sounds like a strategy followed by a person who's trying really, really hard to convince people he's the smartest guy in the room. No, thanks. The universe is far more complex, brilliant, surprising, and mysterious than anything I could conjure up out of sheer genius. I'm not that impressed with myself. I trust that what unfolds before me, unplanned and often miraculous, is going to rock my world. I get giddy about those moments. They're gifts.

6. Assuming you now shoot in what you would consider your natural voice, have you ever wished your voice was different?

The grass is always greener—I have a long list of "wish I made that" pictures. Despite the ridiculous number of photographs in the world, I'm still astonished and inspired by the work artists continue to make. So, yes, I have a voice, and it remains open to change (naturally). Any artist's work reflects a life's history. I'm not who I was twenty years ago, and I sure as hell hope to have learned something twenty years from now. Billie Holiday was always a singular talent with a distinctive voice, but in my mind, she was most breathtaking at the end, when she knew so much that her voice was almost a whisper.

7. How do you know when a body of work is finished?

When my attention wanes and shifts somewhere else, time's up. When I lose that irrational need to do whatever it takes to make the work, then I know it's a wrap.

8. Have you ever had a body of work that was created in the editing process?

Hmm, not entirely. Making films is the closest I've come to this—it's the closest thing to sculpture I've ever done. But I had a very clear rhythm in mind, and a specific intention, before I started editing each film. The process takes a million and one left turns, but with a clear intention, I'm always oriented around this anchor point even when other variables shift.

9. Do you associate your work with a particular genre of photography? If yes, how would you define that genre?

> The obvious thing would be to say portraiture, or landscape, or street photography. Even documentary photography. But I don't associate my work with any of these genres, at least not entirely. I've got one foot in and another foot outside of those genres. I don't play by any inherited rules and I don't go out of my way to break rules unless they need to be broken. I'm quietly radical.

10. Do you ever revisit a series that has already been exhibited or published to shoot more and add to it?

> Yes, just because something has been exhibited, doesn't mean it has to be finished. There are no rules. Or, if there are stupid rules, let's please break them.

11. Do you ever revisit a series that has already been exhibited or published and *reedit* it?

> Always. More often than not, I make a tighter edit. Distance and time can be very valuable, and allow for a detached clearheadedness. Once in a while, though, I rediscover photographs that I'd previously disregarded.

12. Do you create with presentation in mind, be that a gallery show or a book?

> Sometimes I do—with the Boulevard and The 99 portrait series [spontaneous collaborations with strangers on the streets of San Francisco, Hollywood, and the Central Valley], I envisioned them right away as an installation. I saw them as a procession of outliers, a dance macabre that seduces and captivates. ◑

Gregory Halpern

First camera:
I don't remember the make of my first camera, but I do know it was a really crappy thing that cost about $30. I remember loving it to death, though, and being heartbroken when it was stolen out of my dad's glove compartment.

First meaningful photobook:
Triptychs: Buffalo's Lower West Side Revisited (1994) by Milton Rogovin. It's a simple, heartbreaking book that consists of Rogovin revisiting his neighbors every seven or so years to photograph them.

Gregory Halpern (born in Buffalo, New York, 1977) received a BA in history and literature from Harvard University in 1999 and an MFA from California College of the Arts in 2004. In 2014, he became a Guggenheim Fellowship recipient. He has published six books of his work to date: *Harvard Works Because We Do* (2003), *Omaha Sketchbook* (2009), *A* (2011), *East of the Sun, West of the Moon* (in collaboration with Ahndraya Parlato, 2014), *ZZYZX* (2016), and *Confederate Moons* (2018). He is coeditor of *The Photographer's Playbook* (Aperture, 2014) and teaches at the Rochester Institute of Technology.

Personal fact:
As a child I was obsessed with gymnastics and trained (often in my backyard) for up to three hours a day.

1. What comes first for you: the idea for a project, or individual photographs that suggest a concept?

> My answer to this is a little messy, but working through the messiness of that process is part of the joy of fumbling my way toward clarity. It may begin with an idea, but sometimes it's simply a hunch, or a feeling. Or maybe it's an image or a small set of images, a "phrase," if you will, that feels cohesive and unique, which sparks the desire for more. That set may have been made with a conscious intention in mind, but more commonly, it may simply have been the result of an unconscious desire that found its way into existence through the process of making. I don't clearly understand the evolution of the process until the work is done, and I like to take my time working on projects—A [2011] and ZZYZX [2016] each represented about five years of work, respectively. I have often heard novelists say in interviews that they don't know the endings to their books when they begin writing them. Finding out where the work will go is what keeps them going.

> Once I begin to understand what will hold the work together, even if it's just a loose binding structure at first, then I am able to narrow my field of vision, or "material," to whatever is within the parameters of the "project." I really enjoy this phase of working, where I have a sense of where the work is going, without strictly predetermining it. In terms of what material I deem fair game to photograph, I like to allow myself a fairly broad swath of interests—even if they are contradictory or idiosyncratic. Once I have loosely defined parameters, I am free to be as obsessive as possible within that framework. I want parameters narrow enough to make the work compelling and cohesive, but broad enough to allow myself, and my viewer, the pleasure of being able to find their own way through the work.

2. What are the key elements that must be present for you when you are creating a body of work? (Social commentary, strong form, personal connection, photographic reference…)

> I want a strong but loose form, a rough/messy trajectory that is nonetheless compelling. I also want to work toward a challenging kind of beauty, which often means cutting pictures that are too pleasing or uncomplicated. I love Robert Adams's notion from *Why People Photograph* that our objective as artists is to "affirm life without lying about it." I also like a feeling that is perhaps idiosyncratic/ contradictory—simultaneously repulsive and attractive, or unsettling

and reassuring, for example. Making the work has to be pleasurable to me as well, because I am going to spend so much time doing it. Part of that means I need to find a way of working that will provide surprises. If I know exactly what I'm looking for, or exactly what I'm going to find, I'll get bored making the work, and my viewers will get bored looking at it. In some ways, the goal is to make pictures that surprise or even confuse you as a maker. The idea is to *guide* your viewers, but to give them enough space to respect their intelligence as visual readers.

3. Is the idea of a body of work important to you? How does it function in relation to making a great individual photograph?

The idea is essential, both in thinking about my own work and when considering another artist's work. It's inextricably linked to my sense of whether the work is beautiful or not. As for how it functions in relation to making individual photographs, it's hard to say. The act of taking pictures is often an intuitive or unconscious one, but intuition and the unconscious are fed by intellect and the conscious mind. So there is a positive feedback loop—looking at contact sheets informs the conscious mind about what the unconscious is attracted to.

4. Do you have what you might call a "photographic style"?

I have no idea how to answer this one. Sorry!

5. Where would you say your style falls on a continuum between completely intuitive and intellectually formulated?

Both ends of that spectrum are important to me. It's easy to assume that intuition and intellect cannot coexist in work, being that they seem opposing ways of thinking/working, but I believe they can work in tandem and inform one another. I love Sister Corita Kent's "Ten Rules for Students and Teachers," which was popularized by John Cage; Rule #8 is "Do not try to create and analyze at the same time. They are different processes." For me, the act of making pictures tends to lean toward intuition, or sometimes I think of it as (visual) attraction—in that attraction is intuitive or even irrational—whereas editing and sequencing tends, for me, to rely more on intellect. The edit has to serve the larger trajectory of the given project, and because I almost never use text/captions, I need the edit to do a lot of work in terms of conveying ideas. That said, I think it can be helpful to bring intuition back into the editing process (perhaps here "intuition" takes the form of play or surprise) and allow it to influence the edit and the larger concept as a whole.

6. Assuming you now shoot in what you would consider your natural voice, have you ever wished your voice was different?

I have. And I have at times wished an aesthetic or conceptual change would come, but, to me, it feels disingenuous or at least uninteresting to force that change. On the one hand, it's reassuring to feel that you're working in your natural voice, as opposed to a style or voice that is "forced," but on the other hand, you don't want to feel that you are repeating yourself. I think Robert Frank's shift from *The Americans* [1958] to *The Lines of My Hand* [1972], for example, is a fascinating, dramatic shift of voice and style. One senses he *needed* to do that. It's fascinating, to me, to think about the idea of seismic shifts like that. And yet I'm equally fascinated by—and grateful for—someone like Robert Adams, who has remained unwavering and faithful to his original vision.

7. How do you know when a body of work is finished?

It's hard to know. The publication of a book can be a relief, in the sense that there is a deadline past which you can no longer work. There's the danger of tinkering past the point of diminishing returns. Nonetheless, I tend to work slowly, and I like to tinker with an edit and image color for a long time. Too long maybe. I made a book this year, *Confederate Moons* [2018], and although it's small (forty pages), I shot the entire thing in a month, which felt almost recklessly fast, but after so much time on *ZZYZX* I felt the need to make something new. I didn't want to start another five-year project, and I knew there could be something helpful to the creative process in working fast. With slowing down and overthinking, you can talk yourself out of taking risks. And I only continue working on something if I'm still enjoying it. Otherwise it may be time to wrap the project up or just put it on hold while turning attention elsewhere.

8. Have you ever had a body of work that was created in the editing process?

I think so. I think whether a body of work can really sing is often determined by the "finishing" process, which, for me, involves not just editing and sequencing, but decisions about cover and title, which generally come last. *William Eggleston's Guide* [1976] would be a great book no matter how it was sequenced, but I find the day-to-night arc quite beautiful, and I think it suggests a more specific, and darker, vision of Eggleston's Memphis. And the seemingly incongruous insertion of three birds into Richard Billingham's *Ray's a Laugh* [1996] is, I think, a brilliant editing move that turns that book into a truly original work of art. In some ways I think a body of work is always "made" in the editing process. But to begin with, a strong set of images is needed in the first place—enough images so that quite a lot of good images can be thrown out in service of the larger objective, which is to create a cohesive and unique vision.

9. Do you associate your work with a particular genre of photography? If yes, how would you define that genre?

Genres can be frustrating containers at times. They set up boundaries and expectations, both for artist and viewer, and yet they can also be interesting and liberating things to defy. I like that Evans pushed against the term Documentary, for example, calling it Lyric Documentary. I like the films of the Sensory Ethnography Lab at Harvard (particularly *Leviathan*, 2012), and I like their name, which, to me, is a brilliant and perhaps tongue-in-cheek work-around of the problems of the term "documentary." If the genre can't find a new name (I'm thinking of other attempts at qualifying the term, such as Experimental Documentary or Conceptual Documentary) perhaps it will simply be redefined by a new generation of artists; because whatever "it" is happens to include a multitude of profound and powerful ways of working.

Lately I'm fascinated by the genre of Magic Realism. I like to think about what that form might look like photographically, and I think it might sit somewhere between documentary and fantasy. Some suggest that Magic Realism was born out of a response to colonialism, which forced writers to experience two separate realities—that of the conquerors as well as that of the conquered. And so, if we accept this as the origin story of Magic Realism, then the genre as a whole rejects the naive and tyrannical notion that one truth exists—the assumption that earned documentary its bad name in the first place.

One of the things that is simultaneously exciting and troublesome to me about photography is the deception and tension hard-wired into it, the difficulty of defining its slippery relationship to truth. A photograph has potential to be much more objectively truthful/factual than, say, a painting, but painting is more honest about its intentions and possibilities. What I respect, and at times envy, about painting is that it never claims to be anything other than a purely subjective vision. And we place no false expectations on it in terms of its truth value. Photographs, on the other hand, are never entirely fiction or nonfiction.

10. Do you ever revisit a series that has already been exhibited or published to shoot more and add to it?

I never have, but I'm not necessarily opposed to it.

11. Do you ever revisit a series that has already been exhibited or published and *reedit* it?

I did that with my first book, *Harvard Works Because We Do* [2003], which essentially attempted to create a portrait of the university from the perspective of the school's (largely exploited and underpaid) service workers. I was young and knew very little about art when I published it. The book has a lot of text in it, which was presented very traditionally—a single portrait followed by a monologue, or narrative, spoken by the person in the portrait. Years after publishing the book, I realized that when I exhibited the work, if I put an excerpt of the text *inside* the frame (ie, if text and image were printed on the same piece of paper), the text was read quite differently than if it were on the wall *outside* the frame. It was taken much more seriously; it was treated as art, as something to be *interpreted*. It also avoided the traditional image/caption relationship, where text is used to *explain* the image and in the process shuts down readers' potential to interpret the image for themselves. It was such a simple revelation, but it was important and exciting to me to be able to re-present the work this way.

12. Do you create with presentation in mind, be that a gallery show or a book?

I tend to think in book form. Sometimes I wish I thought more for the wall, because a good show can be an incredible experience, but I have to admit that I just love books more. First off, a big wall and big white space are challenging for me, in part, because the options are so limitless. Plus, there is the fact that my experiences in galleries are often clouded by so much else—the semi-publicness of the space, an atmosphere of exclusion or pretention, or the distracting and unsettling reminder that most galleries function as stores for the super-rich. I'm partial to the democracy and intimacy of experiencing an artist's vision in book form—if you own the book, you can experience it whenever you want and in the comfort of your own home. And from a creative standpoint, I actually like the limitations of the book form—a fixed size, sequence, etc.—and I like how you can control the viewer's experience. A book is typically a complete and contextualized representation of an artist's vision, and I love the directness and democracy of that exchange, from the artist's mind into my hands. ◑

Halpern

"I believe photographing people forces an interest in lives other than our own, allowing an opportunity to see ourselves reflected in someone else."

Curran Hatleberg

First camera:
Canon AE-1, lent to me by my uncle

First meaningful photobook:
The Americans (1958) by
Robert Frank

Curran Hatleberg (born in Washington, DC, 1982) received
his MFA from Yale University School of Art in 2010. He is a
recipient of a Magnum Emergency Fund grant, an Aaron Siskind
Foundation Individual Photographer's Fellowship, and a Richard
Benson Prize for excellence in photography. Hatleberg has taught
photography at numerous institutions, including Yale University
School of Art and Cooper Union. Among his books are his debut
monograph *Lost Coast* (2016) and *Somewhere Someone* (in
collaboration with Cynthia Daignault, 2017). He lives and works
in Baltimore.

First meaningful exhibition:
When I was about ten years old
my uncle took me to the Walter
De Maria Earth Room [Dia Art
Foundation] in New York City.
I remember the heavy smell of
dirt was intoxicating, and the air
was moist and cool. I couldn't
believe anything so illogical and
magical could possibly exist.

Personal Fact:
When I was a child, the only way my
parents could get me to fall asleep
was to put me in the car and drive
around the block. Maybe it was the
sound of tires on cement, or the rush
of the wind pouring in that sedated me.
Perhaps this is an origin story, why my
work is still so much about driving.

1. What comes first for you: the idea for a project, or individual photographs that suggest a concept?

     The individual photograph always comes first.

2. What are the key elements that must be present for you when you are creating a body of work? (Social commentary, strong form, personal connection, photographic reference…)

     My work relies on personal connection, and I have built my life around spending time with people in places that are unknown to me. One of the pleasures of photographing people is in not knowing what's going to happen. Human beings have the shocking ability to be entirely predictable one minute and completely surprising the next. I remember a woman who invited me to stay with her for a few nights. "It's dangerous out there," she warned. She was an incredible cook and fed me like I was her son. One night we ate spaghetti on paper plates in front of the TV. When a strong wind blasted into the room, she fired a pistol out the door into the night. I didn't even know she had a gun. She never mentioned it. One of the shots missed the open door and left a ragged hole in the wood paneling. She rocked out of her recliner as if nothing had happened. Smiling, she warmly insisted I have seconds. I believe photographing people forces an interest in lives other than our own, allowing an opportunity to see ourselves reflected in someone else. Biases, judgments, and stereotypes fall away in the face of vivid experience.

3. Is the idea of a body of work important to you? How does it function in relation to making a great individual photograph?

     I am deeply interested in the rise and fall of narrative sequence. However, I never set out imagining a body of work. Instead, the process begins with singular, impactful pictures. For an individual image to be great, it must have the essential components—the right light, composition, mood, and technical execution—but really that's all secondary. To me, aesthetic harmony means very little unless the photograph reveals a personal, emotional truth. I want a viewer to feel like they're inside the experience rather than looking at it. I want each picture to be strong enough to stand on its own. I know it may sound strange talking about truth after more than one hundred years of questioning photography's veracity, but I'm aiming for a fiction that is more real than reality.

4. Do you have what you might call a "photographic style"?

I say "Yes" to everything to see what happens. When I'm photographing I agree to almost every single thing. My work depends on it. I meet people by chance, and I surrender control. I rely on my subjects to direct and shape the moments I will record. I can never guess where they might take me, who they might show me, or what they might choose to reveal of themselves. In the company of strangers I wait for a picture without knowing what it will be or when it will show itself. I never know what is going to happen until it's already underway. I've found that if I'm hesitant or scared about making a photograph but still mesmerized by the thought of it, that's usually a good sign that I've reached a starting point. Every relationship starts because a person fascinates me. I'm under their spell for one reason or another. Maybe a stranger's face reminds me of someone else I know but can't remember. Maybe they are unusual and alone. Maybe they are walking down the highway in the rain, yelling at the sky. Usually this magnetism happens naturally and with a sense that there could be some mystery to uncover—something to shake out and bring to light.

5. Where would you say your style falls on a continuum between completely intuitive and intellectually formulated?

When I'm photographing, it's as if I am looking for something that's missing, but I'm not sure what it is. As if I am on the verge of something important that keeps eluding me. All my pictures originate from a curiosity, a desire to experience things and express that wonder. If there is any construct behind my work, it is getting in the car and driving. I'd say, especially in America, that the concept of being on the road is an intellectual construct in itself. My work always begins with driving, following an imaginary line that I make up as I go. At the beginning of a project I don't have any plan at all. There's no way of knowing where I'll go or whom I'll meet. I let chance and intuition steer me to a place I would never go otherwise. There's no preexisting agenda involved, just the pull of the moment until something grabs my attention and snaps my brain into focus. I just wait. I wait and drive and pray for the story to begin. Then I wait some more. I don't choose what kind of story it is or what's going to happen, but when the door opens up, I go all the way in.

6. Assuming you now shoot in what you would consider your natural voice, have you ever wished your voice was different?

I don't think so, although I'd say that most artists start out by copying the voices of their idols and mentors. That's just inexperience and worship at work. It's nearly impossible to make something original. So, yes, when I first picked up a camera, I wished I had a different artistic voice—but I just didn't know what I was interested in yet. I hadn't put in the time to develop my own ideas, so I defaulted to imitating the successes of the people I loved. Eventually every artist has to overcome the anxiety of influence, but it's hard to love the artist that you are, not the one you want to be. An artist must take from tradition without being bound to it. I still page through the monographs of my heroes regularly, if only to remind myself how exceptional a work of art can be, and of how much farther I still have to go.

7. How do you know when a body of work is finished?

I don't think an artist ever gets to decide when something's finished. There's never enough time, never enough resolution or assurance. The shadow of an ending falls over you whether you like it or not. When I was living in Eureka, California, I remember struggling to finish Lost Coast [2016]. My problem was a deadline. I had never worked with a time constraint before, or an audience, and suddenly the joy of working had vanished. Even though I had already shot hundreds of rolls of film, facing a deadline I was now convinced the project needed something more than I already had. This worry put me into a state of frenzy. I was moving back East when the project ended, and I was frantic to get more solid material before I left, even if I had to force it. I was running out of time quickly.

Over the following weeks I had a hard time making something happen. I was utterly distressed until one wet day I ended up down at the waterfront. The place was an abandoned mess. The scene made no impression on my mind at all. No people around to meet. There was no picture here. Through a shiny mist I walked toward the edge of the Pacific with my camera. When I passed a parked van I was startled to see a dog I hadn't noticed before. The dog was large and dirty, and when we locked eyes I noticed it was missing one. Before I knew what was happening I was on the ground while the dog shook my leg between its teeth. I struck wildly at its face, trying to break its grip, but my blows only seemed to encourage its resolve. When my jeans tore open I saw blood. The whole scene played before me at a slow, dreamlike pace. Suddenly, without warning the dog trotted away out of sight and disappeared behind a fence. I lay on my back with my eyes closed, for what felt like a long time. The light was changing fast. The tide was going out. I drove out of town forever the next day. I hadn't known it before, but the project was already finished.

8. Have you ever had a body of work that was created in the editing process?

Yes. I don't look over anything until I've shot hundreds of rolls. When at last I do review what I have, my editing process is entirely intuitive—pure trial and error. I look over what assets I have then I make gut decisions. What I find and don't find influences the next round of shooting. What's confusing is that in a stack of negatives there are infinite stories that can be told, and I can never know if I picked the best one. At a certain point, you realize the pictures are in charge and you just have to let go.

To complicate things further, I often hit a wall because I'm incapable of seeing the images with any impartiality—the memory of being there in the moment always overrides any true objectivity. Occasionally when I'm photographing I find myself inside an experience that feels like the entire mystery of the world is contained in that present moment. Later, I end up questioning whether the reason I'm drawn to a picture is only because the experience I had was meaningful. Over time certain images will claim importance in my mind. They develop a nagging insistence and won't be ignored. From these, one or two foundational pieces an idea starts to reveal itself. These are the images that become the skeletal organization of the book. Pretty soon pictures start to link up and fill in the gaps, and I find a rhythm. Picture by picture, a narrative takes shape.

9. Do you associate your work with a particular genre of photography? If yes, how would you define that genre?

There are certainly people that I feel a kinship with—but that transcends traditional genres. In general, I find myself uncomfortable with labels, as those often only reinforce a misguided preconception or stereotype about the art. Often classification closes down part of the creative interpretation. I don't like boundaries. I'd rather let the work speak for itself. Remove the baggage of category, and the photograph deepens and opens up to interpretation.

10. Do you ever revisit a series that has already been exhibited or published to shoot more and add to it?

> Yes. Sometimes the show happens before the book does. I don't consider the body of work done until the book is made. Unlike a show, which is impermanent, a book is indelible. It's this permanence that makes a book so important to me.

11. Do you ever revisit a series that has already been exhibited or published and *reedit* it?

> At this point in my career I haven't, but it's still early, and I can't predict what will happen in the long future. I can't imagine doing it, as the work feels over once it's published, and there is no way to go back in time to where and when I shot it—to be that person, in that moment, again. But who knows?

12. Do you create with presentation in mind, be that a gallery show or a book?

> Presentation is always decided at the end, at the very end. ◑

Todd Hido

First camera:
Nikon FM

First meaningful photobook:
The Americans (1958) by
Robert Frank

Todd Hido (born in Kent, Ohio, 1968) received his BFA from
Tufts University in 1991 and his MFA from California College of
the Arts in 1996, where he now is an adjunct professor. Hido has
published over a dozen books, including *House Hunting* (2001),
Roaming (2004), *Excerpts from Silver Meadows* (2013), *Intimate
Distance: Twenty-Five Years of Photographs, A Chronological
Album* (Aperture, 2016), and *Bright Black World* (2018). In 2014,
Aperture published *Todd Hido on Landscapes, Interiors, and the
Nude* as part of The Photography Workshop series. Hido is based
in the San Francisco Bay Area.

First meaningful exhibition:
1988 *Carnegie International*,
Carnegie Museum of Art, Pittsburgh

Personal fact:
In 2005 I learned that my vision
was "like the wallpaper in an old
abandoned house, falling off the walls
slowly but surely." If we did not act
immediately I might have gone blind.
All I could imagine was the kind of
room Francesca Woodman liked to
work in! I now walk around with a
silicone clip embedded into my head,
which holds my eyeball together. It's
not quite bionic, but I see perfectly.

1. What comes first for you: the idea for a project, or individual photographs that suggest a concept?

> I always find the concepts in my work through making pictures and sorting them out, which clarifies my ideas. Most often I am using my intuition up front. The process of analyzing comes later.

2. What are the key elements that must be present for you when you are creating a body of work? (Social commentary, strong form, personal connection, photographic reference…)

> Personal connections and emotional resonance are absolutely essential elements in order to stay engaged in a body of work for the length of time it takes to actually create something worthwhile. Form is a given; it needs to be great. It is something we can't do without and is a basic need for visual communication. Also, my mind naturally pulls toward narrative, so that's another key element that I can't live without.

3. Is the idea of a body of work important to you? How does it function in relation to making a great individual photograph?

> Yes, having a body of work is important. But I have a very simple policy regarding my photographs: "All killer, no filler." Each and every image that I make (whether it is a stand-alone or made to exist within a series) will not see the light of day unless it meets my very stringent criteria, which is that each picture needs to be able to stand by itself.

> These strong images then become the structural framework of a cohesive body of work. Photography is serial in nature, and oftentimes a group of pictures becomes a much deeper thing than a gathering of single images.

4. Do you have what you might call a "photographic style"?

> Yes, as I believe all photographers do, to one degree or another. It's something everyone who has taught any kind of art class has seen: you direct a diverse group of students to photograph or draw or paint the exact same thing, and they come back with wildly different styles. The personal always seeps through.

> It can, of course, take years to refine that style, but at its core, it is something that is unconscious and automatic, and I feel very lucky

to have my own refined style. I can photograph people and places, at night or in the daytime, and somehow it all remains consistent. I think it comes from trusting one's instincts and also from dependably using the same materials and equipment.

5. Where would you say your style falls on a continuum between completely intuitive and intellectually formulated?

My style is fundamentally intuitive. I'm not so sure if I trust the idea of an intellectual construct of a style. For me, style is such a personal and spontaneous thing—when you formulate it in advance, instead of allowing it to occur organically over time, it can become thin and flimsy.

6. Assuming you now shoot in what you would consider your natural voice, have you ever wished your voice was different?

I have never actually considered this possibility. You can reinvent aspects of yourself to some degree, but the innate you always lingers.

7. How do you know when a body of work is finished?

I used to say, "When I stop getting out of the car to take the picture." Basically, you know you're finished when the burden of setting up the camera outweighs your drive to capture that particular image.

One note of caution: I feel that photographers and artists these days are very much on an accelerated production cycle where we can feel pressured to have an entirely new project every couple of years. It is important to slow down around your own work, trust yourself, and ask if you *really* are done. Knowing when to push through and keep going is just as important as knowing when to stop. The new iterations, the small discoveries, and the nuances of my own way of working were all important realizations for me, and those only came through continued efforts.

After I published two books of houses at night [*House Hunting*, 2001; *Outskirts*, 2002], which fed into numerous solo shows of that work, it could have easily made sense to move on to something different. Yet I continued to make that work at almost the same pace as when I had first stumbled upon the subject matter, for the simple reason that I was still drawn to it. Ten years later, when I had the opportunity to do a large-scale installation at Pier 24 Photography in San Francisco, the fact that I had kept with the project meant that I had enough work to have images wrapped around the entire room. The volume of images was quite important in making that installation truly effective; otherwise, the photographs would have been swallowed up by the empty space. If I had stopped "getting out of the car," as it were, the show would never have been possible.

8. Have you ever had a body of work that was created in the editing process?

That is an excellent question because of the serial nature of photography. As photographers, we go out and shoot, make new images, gather and collect, and obsessively repeat the same motions over and over again. The result yields many more images than you can use. But then whole strains of work can emanate from searching through piles of "extra" images. My book *A Road Divided* [2010] was created like this. It's not even that the work is *created* through the editing process as much as it *reveals* itself to you through the editing process. Or at least exposes the themes that your mind has been churning over subconsciously.

9. Do you associate your work with a particular genre of photography? If yes, how would you define that genre?

Not necessarily, though I do think back to earlier in my career when I tried to understand where my work would fit into the history of the entire medium. I think it is important for a young photographer to know what has come before them, in order to not be derivative.

I often suggest to my students that they ask themselves, "Where is my place in this artistic continuum, and how do I make a meaningful contribution to the medium?"

10. Do you ever revisit a series that has already been exhibited or published to shoot more and add to it?

Yes, definitely. As I earlier noted, my photographs of houses at night were truly an ongoing series, even though I have two published monographs and many exhibitions of that work. Yet I still am compelled to take those images when I come across them. I believe that photographing houses at night will be something I continue to do my entire career. One thing that is very interesting is that most of those images were made on film, and as digital technology has grown, it is quite interesting to revisit the night with a much more sensitive and responsive tool.

11. Do you ever revisit a series that has already been exhibited or published and *reedit* it?

Yes, constantly. Photography has this special quality embedded within it that makes it even more glorious and important the older it gets. We change as people, and the world changes around us, so the meaning and interpretation of our images necessarily shift as well, even for the artist who originally made them.

Reconsidering a series with the benefit of the passage of time enriches the existing images beautifully. Stephen Shore's expansion of *Uncommon Places* [1982, 2004, 2015] and Rineke Dijkstra's recent *WO MEN* [2017] are two excellent examples of this.

12. Do you create with presentation in mind, be that a gallery show or a book?

There are three parts of photography: shooting, selecting, and presenting. They are all equally important, but I never take a picture thinking about how it is going to hang on a wall. When I get to the organization and selection of images, at that point, I absolutely do that part with presentation in mind.

You ask about photobooks as well, and though I've had some gallery and museum show installations of which I am incredibly proud, for me the photobook is the purest form of presentation.

I started obsessively collecting photobooks when I was eighteen, and I like to think about my library as an organic resource that I can constantly be inspired by. I frequently leave books open around the house. Some books get put away soon after, or the page gets turned to a different image, depending on my mood. But certain books have been left open to the same page, the same image, for years, because the photograph is just *that* good.

The art historian Alexander Nemerov recently did me the immense honor of writing a preface to my book *Bright Black World* [2018]. The entire essay is gorgeous, and makes me proud to be an artist, but I especially love this sentence related to books, which rises to the level of poetry: "Back on the leveled ground of this book, the reader examines the pictures in private devotion, running her fingers on empty fields." It perfectly describes the photobook experience: intimate, tactile, democratic. ◑

"An individual photograph is like a single cell, or a single voice; I think that a body of work comes into being when those individual elements constellate and resonate with one another."

Rinko Kawauchi

First camera:
Canon F-1

First meaningful photobook:
Sally Mann's *Immediate Family* (1992)

Rinko Kawauchi (born in Shiga, Japan, 1972) earned a degree from Seian University of Art and Design, Otsu, Japan, in 1993. In 2001, she launched her career with the simultaneous publication of three volumes: *Utatane*, *Hanabi*, and *Hanako*. Since then, she has published more than twenty books of her work, including three with Aperture: *Illuminance* (2011), *Ametsuchi* (2013), and *Halo* (2017). She has received the Kimura Ihei Photography Award and the International Center of Photography Infinity Award in Art, and in 2012, she was one of four artists shortlisted for the Deutsche Börse Photography Prize. Kawauchi lives and works in Tokyo.

Kawauchi

First meaningful exhibition:
W. Eugene Smith, in Osaka or Kyoto, in 1993

Personal fact:
When I was four years old, my family moved from the countryside to a town. I wanted to go back to our previous house, but it was impossible. This was the first time I realized that I couldn't go back to the past, and it changed my life.

1. What comes first for you: the idea for a project, or individual photographs that suggest a concept?

> Most of the time the photographs tend to be a prelude to the concept. With my earlier works *Utatane* and *Hanabi* [both 2001], for example, I carefully selected photographs to use from the pool I had accumulated after a number of years of shooting—all the while thinking about how to structure the pages of a book. To bring each to completion, at the end I went out and photographed additional shots to create the imagery I wanted to depict. For *Halo* [2017], a more recent work, I felt that I could achieve the desired aesthetic by amalgamating photographs I had taken for different projects—culminating in compiling the series into book form.

2. What are the key elements that must be present for you when you are creating a body of work? (Social commentary, strong form, personal connection, photographic reference...)

> First, that the body of work connects to me personally—and to my own latent mind and subconscious. From there, I hope that eventually it will resonate with others and with society at large.

3. Is the idea of a body of work important to you? How does it function in relation to making a great individual photograph?

> An individual photograph is like a single cell, or a single voice; I think that a body of work comes into being when those individual elements constellate and resonate with one another.

4. Do you have what you might call a "photographic style"?

> Maybe I do. I'm not really sure. I'm in constant contemplation of how I can create and depict things in a way that is entirely unique to me. All in all, I would say that this process gives way to my photographic style.

5. Where would you say your style falls on a continuum between completely intuitive and intellectually formulated?

> I think that my photographic style is very much based on intuition.

6. Assuming you now shoot in what you would consider your natural voice, have you ever wished your voice was different?

> Not particularly, but there are times when I'm making new works that I feel that I want to try approaching things from a different perspective.

7. How do you know when a body of work is finished?

> When the discourse between myself and the work has, by and large, reached a conclusion.

8. Have you ever had a body of work that was created in the editing process?

> Yes, I have. In a way different from viewing a single photograph on its own, another world comes into view when lining up photographs of varying subjects. The overall "countenance" of a work can be expressed in a variety of ways depending on how one arranges these components; as such, the editing process is crucial. It is also an entertaining one, as elements I had not been conscious of while shooting often come into view when editing.

9. Do you associate your work with a particular genre of photography? If yes, how would you define that genre?

> I'm not sure if my work fits within a particular genre. I utilize photography as a mode of expression; in my works, I want to depict subject matter that only photography is capable of capturing, in a way that only I am capable of rendering. In that sense, maybe I could say that I aim to create works that fall into a sort of hybrid category—one that remains free of genre typology.

10. Do you ever revisit a series that has already been exhibited or published to shoot more and add to it?

> Not often, but I do from time to time. There are also projects that I want to do over again. Taking my work *Hanabi*, which focused on the dance of light and colors of fireworks, as an example, sometimes I feel myself wanting to shoot an entirely new collection of photographs and to completely re-create the series. With *Cui Cui* [2005], which depicts my own family, a part of me wants to add more images and to reconstruct the work.

Kawauchi

11. Do you ever revisit a series that has already been exhibited or published and *reedit* it?

> I've almost never revisited or reedited a past series before, but there are a few published works that I would like to try recompiling and publishing again, if I get the chance. For example, as noted above, I've continued shooting and adding onto *Hanabi* and *Cui Cui* postpublication, so I'd like to reedit these works someday.

12. Do you create with presentation in mind, be that a gallery show or a book?

> Yes, I often do. Many of my works in the past were created with their final book form in mind, but in the case of more recent works like *Ametsuchi* [2013] and *Halo*, my plans for how to display them in exhibition form actually came first. There are times in such cases that I'm required to narrow down the materials or cameras I'm able to use, but even if the idea of how to exhibit the works at a gallery show precedes the works themselves, it doesn't really have a significant impact on my creative process. ◑

Peter Kayafas

First camera:
Canon Canonet QL17

First meaningful photobook:
Let Us Now Praise Famous Men (Walker Evans and James Agee, 1941). Made me go on the road to see for myself.

Peter Kayafas (born in Boston, 1971) is a photographer, publisher, curator, and teacher who lives in New York, where he is the director of the Eakins Press Foundation. He has taught photography at Pratt Institute in Brooklyn since 2000. In addition to *The Merry Cemetery of Sapanta* (2007), *O Public Road! Photographs of America* (2009), and *Totems* (2012), his most recent monograph, *The Way West* (2019), is available from his imprint Purple Martin Press. Kayafas earned a BFA in photography from the Tisch School of the Arts, NYU, in 1993. He is a recipient of a 2019 Guggenheim Fellowship.

First meaningful exhibition:
The Helen Levitt show at the Met, in 1992. Helen Levitt was there. They showed her film *In the Street* (1948), which she made with James Agee and Janice Loeb. The show was curated by Sandy Phillips and Maria Morris Hambourg.

Personal fact:
I received my first camera at the age of two and had my first show at the age of four at the Massachusetts College of Art and Design (where my father had established the undergraduate photography program).

1. What comes first for you: the idea for a project, or individual photographs that suggest a concept?

> I approach my interaction with the world through the camera without much preconception. It's important to me that "projects" such as they are (or might become) evolve out of using the camera without being inhibited by the preoccupation to hunt something down that fits with a project. To be too preoccupied with one project inevitably precludes the discovery of another.
>
> In fact, some projects don't present themselves until substantial time has gone by since the making of what become the first core pictures of that series. In such cases, it is the emergence of a pattern in the work that calls for it to be considered and pursued in a specific way.
>
> I think of using the camera over a lifetime as one long project, one epic journey, out of which multiple smaller or larger projects evolve when they command specific momentum.

2. What are the key elements that must be present for you when you are creating a body of work? (Social commentary, strong form, personal connection, photographic reference…)

> A body of work should embody and depict a journey toward knowledge, the beginning, middle, and end of which collectively demonstrate an arc of experience. The most important single factor in the finished body of work is that I must be able to see the evolution of a visual vocabulary and know something more about the subject(s), both in a specific sense (ie, my relationship to the subject) and in a more general sense (ie, my relationship to the human condition).
>
> If I have a sense of responsibility for my work as a photographer, it is to the process and to the subject simultaneously. If a viewer finds politics present in my work, or personal resonance, or the reinforcement of a social agenda, then I have partially succeeded in my goal to make pictures that are simultaneously about something specific while leaving enough room for interpretation.

3. Is the idea of a body of work important to you? How does it function in relation to making a great individual photograph?

A body of work is a necessary part of the important process of creating tangible, measurable milestones in the evolution of my own cumulative visual knowledge. Of course, individual photographs are the essential components of the process—the whole point, really—and I strive for strong individual photographs to be the guideposts to which I look for direction about what constitutes a project and, subsequently, a finished body of work. To be truly excited by an individual photograph, and then a series of photographs that when strung together become greater than the sum of their parts, is the principal goal I have for my work.

4. Do you have what you might call a "photographic style"?

My photographic style has already been defined over a long period of time by people who work in similar ways. Terms like "social documentary," "documentary style," and "social landscape" all intend to do something similar in defining a style. But this question brings up an interesting point: Does photographic style refer to the way that a photographer works, or the results? It may be a bit too semantic, but I think that a lot of photographers work with similar intellectual or philosophical pretexts, and end up with pictures that look very different from the pictures of others who work in a similar photographic style.

5. Where would you say your style falls on a continuum between completely intuitive and intellectually formulated?

I would like to think that it starts from a nearly completely intuitive place that subsequently benefits from the context of a more intellectually formulated construct. In other words, recognizing a pattern in my work is an acknowledgment of the important role that intuition plays; what I do with that recognition, how I pursue the "project," and how the project is presented as a body of work is my version of the "intellectually formulated construct."

My agenda is not simply to find what I am looking for, but to really see—to allow myself to be surprised by the people and the places, and especially by the photographs I make. This approach has liberated my process from the burden of preconception. I have an abiding faith in the power of photography, when applied with conscious concern in a focused way over a long period of time, to reveal essential aspects of humanity that would otherwise remain camouflaged in caricature.

6. Assuming you now shoot in what you would consider your natural voice, have you ever wished your voice was different?

I think an artist's goal should not be to find a voice per se, but to empower the one that he or she already has. This is not to say that an artist should not strive to challenge and refine his or her voice, but I think that there is nothing more dangerous to original work than trying to create a voice. Sometimes one's voice resonates with others, sometimes it doesn't—but if one cannot hear and acknowledge one's own voice in the work that they do, they are lost.

It can be frustrating to hear that the work one is making looks like the work of others, but I think that starting out trying to be original (rather than true) virtually ensures that the work will be stylistically incoherent. Originality lies in the embrace of one's own voice, not in the reaction to others' voices. The harder we try to sound original, the less like ourselves we sound. Rather than that my voice was different, I would say that I sometimes wish my voice was more broadly heard.

7. How do you know when a body of work is finished?

I think it is essential to finish, to edit and present, in whatever form, a project or body of work so that it is permanent, out of the hands of the artist, and into the public sphere. Completing anything well requires layers of consideration and hard work—including an engaged process of distillation—and embodies factors of intention and rigor that give important context to a group of photographs. Finished works also become valuable bellwethers and milestones in the continued growth of an artist.

There's an analogy that I have found useful in my teaching in which I compare the finishing of projects to the act of rock-climbing. During a free-climb, the climber scales a cliff face without the safety of ropes for much of the journey upward, unlike a more traditional climb, where a belay is secured at the top. As the free-climber reaches certain points, they place an anchor and attach the rope connected to their harness before proceeding. This ensures that, in the event of a fall from a higher point, the climber won't fall farther than the point of the last anchor. A finished project is a little like an anchor: it provides a point of reference and the ability to see how far one has progressed (or not). And, during any period of doubt about one's voice as an artist, the anchor/finished project represents the furthest point that one can fall/regress to.

When I look back on any project that I have finished, whether it be from a few years or a few decades ago, I find that there are always things I'm proud of, as well as things I would do totally differently. It seems to me that there is no better indication of growth as an artist than to have circumstances that allow for such insights.

Recognizing when a project is finished is a complicated and fraught thing, and for some projects this point is much clearer than for others. For instance, one way that a project is clearly finished is if the subject matter is no longer available or accessible. For other projects, it is a cyclical evolution. At a certain point, the dynamic cycle of editing the pictures I have in hand and then adding to them with new work begins to take shape and feel complete. When it feels complete, I shift my energies to making the strongest edit and presentation. In this process, it can be invaluable to have another set of trained eyes involved, someone who understands the work, but who ideally also possesses the ability to be candid about what doesn't work in the presentation.

8. Have you ever had a body of work that was created in the editing process?

I think that there are bodies of work that could be extracted from my archive, though I've not yet done much of that. Because the meaning of photographs changes according to our relationship to them at any given moment, aspects that might not have been obvious when the pictures were made can become apparent as time goes by. How often do we recognize in a picture not so much what is present, but what is absent? How often do we experience the power of a work of art not so much for what it depicts, but for what it means, which is increasingly, with the passing of time, essentially our awareness of how much different things are now.

Perhaps the greatest strength of any photographer is their ability to see clearly what is relevant in front of their camera and act with the faith that it will only become more so with time. This basic fact advocates for regular reconsideration of archival work.

9. Do you associate your work with a particular genre of photography? If yes, how would you define that genre?

> I think that genres of photography are constantly being redefined, though the definitions of the nature of certain approaches to process, especially to the act of making photographs, remain fairly consistent. My approach has always been based on the belief that the world is much more interesting to me than any preconceptions I may have about it, and that the camera is the perfect tool to explore, celebrate, and memorialize this fact. I'd like to think that with my photographs I am collaborating with accident. In this sense, my work comes from the world I photograph, not the other way around. There are obviously many other photographers, since the earliest practitioners of the medium, who have felt and acted similarly. In this way, I think that "photographic style" is analogous to "genre."

10. Do you ever revisit a series that has already been exhibited or published to shoot more and add to it?

> The bulk of the work that I have done for the past thirty years comes from traveling in the United States and photographing the rituals and essential character of the people in particular regions. In this process, I have finished numerous projects, completed several books, and exhibited finished bodies of work. I still spend substantial amounts of time every year traveling and making new work. So, yes, I guess I am constantly revisiting and adding to work that has already been exhibited. I cannot imagine ever being in a situation where I would say to myself: "I can't make this picture because that project is finished." That would be a violation of the most basic tenets of my approach to photography.

11. Do you ever revisit a series that has already been exhibited or published and *reedit* it?

> One of the most important facts about finished work is that it cannot be reedited. That said, there's nothing to keep particular images that have been included in finished projects from being repurposed or recontextualized in other bodies of work. Sometimes a single picture from a past book or exhibition can be the beginning of a new project. In fact, it is the case with almost every body of work that I have finished that one or several ideas contained therein functioned as the seed germ for another project.

12. Do you create with presentation in mind, be that a gallery show or a book?

I have never consciously made a photograph with its end point in mind. It is almost always the case that any picture of mine that is seen by anyone other than myself ends up in a publication, on a wall, or on the internet—or, more often than not, all three. But, since I do not make photographs with one of these venues in mind, the final vehicle for my work does not have any conscious bearing on the making of the pictures themselves. ◑

"My work is a process of making, thinking, and then remaking. The process reveals unconscious wishes, things I didn't even know I was thinking about."

Justine Kurland

First camera:
Nikon F2

First meaningful photobook:
Josef Koudelka's *Gypsies* (1975)

Justine Kurland (born in Warsaw, New York, 1969) received her BFA from the School of Visual Arts in 1996 and her MFA from the Yale University School of Art in 1998. In 2013, she was awarded a New York Foundation of the Arts Artists' Fellowship for Photography. Her publications include *Spirit West* (2000), *Another Girl, Another Planet* (2001), *Old Joy* (with Jonathan Raymond, 2004), *This Train Is Bound for Glory* (2009), *Sincere Auto Care* (2014), *Black Threads from Meng Chiao* (with John Yau, 2015), *Highway Kind* (Aperture, 2016), and *Girl Pictures* (2018). She lives and works in New York.

Personal fact:
I wanted to photograph someone from the 1970s counter-culture Rainbow Family's secret Tribe of Elders. After a lot of searching I found one of them, an old biker from Missoula. When we met he offered to take me sightseeing in the mountains. On the drive he recounted the story of beginning the Rainbow gatherings to welcome home Vietnam Vets who "couldn't get chicks to sleep with them." That's when he stopped the car, "Let me give you a hug, Sister." He stuck his snake tongue in my mouth and, with a surprisingly strong grip, pushed my head down and dry humped my face through his dirty overalls until I managed to right myself. All he said was, "I needed that," and then started up the car like nothing happened. I left town without photographing him.

1. What comes first for you: the idea for a project, or individual photographs that suggest a concept?

    > My work is a process of making, thinking, and then remaking. The process reveals unconscious wishes, things I didn't even know I was thinking about. At the same time, I'm building a relationship with my subject and form, which generates new approaches. But the concepts and making are intertwined and simultaneous.

2. What are the key elements that must be present for you when you are creating a body of work? (Social commentary, strong form, personal connection, photographic reference...)

    > I care most about how things feel. I forgot who said photography strives for the condition of music; it animates the space between the viewer and the art object. By giving shape to how things feel I hope my photographs are relatable, and can form lines of connection and belonging. Affect is not directly political but is in close proximity. It is the cry of the people rather than the policy that tears them apart.

3. Is the idea of a body of work important to you? How does it function in relation to making a great individual photograph?

    > I tend to privilege the whole over the parts. But it's not always true that the whole is larger than the parts. Take the example of a fox: her tail is certainly larger than her whole. It's funny to think of a body of work, as though certain pieces were a leg and another the nose. And with the camera body our options expand—the phallic lens and the womblike interior chamber.

    > I imagine a body of work as a series of great individual photographs. Sometimes they follow each other in a logical progression, and sometimes they digress. A series of photographs form a constellation where the space in between can be as significant as each picture.

4. Do you have what you might call a "photographic style"?

    > *Style* is a tricky word. It's something you can be in or out of. And then there is applied style, as in the flavor of a frozen TV dinner. I asked a writer friend to define *style*, and he said it was the symptom of deficiency —it's all the hemming and hawing around writing something perfectly.

Critics have identified my style as Yale Girl Photography, but a childhood friend who knows me better says my style is Coffee Stain.

5. Where would you say your style falls on a continuum between completely intuitive and intellectually formulated?

When I was a younger artist I staged my photographs. But compared to other practitioners of staged narratives, my production was low and my directorial hand relaxed. I wanted to let the narratives unravel. I eventually stopped staging the pictures altogether. I became more interested in letting chance and accident intervene. But I still consider the photographs to be narrative. With a 4-by-5 camera you're not grabbing pictures, it involves a tripod and a mostly still subject. So no matter how intuitively I shoot, they are always formulated constructions.

6. Assuming you now shoot in what you would consider your natural voice, have you ever wished your voice was different?

I distrust the word *natural*, especially in relation to photography. One of photography's most insidious characteristics is how it tends to naturalize what it describes as fact. I believe in nurture before nature. My education came through John Szarkowski's canon of mostly white men, their syntax and grammar. Adrienne Rich describes the problem and inevitability of speaking in the language of the oppressor in her essay "When We Dead Awaken." I both love and reject my voice.

7. How do you know when a body of work is finished?

I teach with Nayland Blake, and I have heard him tell students, "Finishing is for furniture." Once the problems of construction are resolved, of a table for instance, the process no longer involves thinking. Finishing is the stage where the person mindlessly applies polish but no longer pays attention. At this point you are no longer making art. Nayland is one of the most intelligent and clear-sighted artists I know. I often ask myself, "What would Nayland do?"

8. Have you ever had a body of work that was created in the editing process?

You could describe almost every work of photography as a process of arrangement and editing. Framing is a type of editing. For my work, the choices of what to keep and what to leave out happen before and after the shutter is released.

Kurland

9. Do you associate your work with a particular genre of photography? If yes, how would you define that genre?

I associate my work with the artists I am indebted to: Dayanita Singh, Zoe Leonard, Carrie Mae Weems, Valie Export, Moyra Davey, Jennifer Montgomery, Betty Tompkins, LaToya Ruby Frazier, Sharon Hayes, Susan Lipper, Hannah Wilke, Anna Craycroft, Jay DeFeo, Katherine Hubbard, and Emily Roysdon.

My work is in alignment with Valerie Solanas's *SCUM Manifesto* [1967]: "The true artist is every self-confident, healthy female, and in a female society the only Art, the only Culture, will be conceited, kooky, funky, females grooving on each other and on everything else in the universe."

10. Do you ever revisit a series that has already been exhibited or published to shoot more and add to it?

My work doesn't stop and start when I have an exhibition. And the terms of making don't stay fixed in between shows. My work evolves irrespective of my exhibition schedule. But I am consciously trying to push myself along, letting the evolution of the work respond to the questions proposed by my previous pieces as much as by the circumstances of my life. From a distance you can see trajectories between staged to documentary, from looking outward to looking inward, as well as a shifting sphere of influence.

11. Do you ever revisit a series that has already been exhibited or published and *reedit* it?

I just did for the first time. I exhibited a complete set of vintage prints of the first series I was known for, Girl Pictures [1997, 2002, published in book form in 2018]. I traveled across the country staging photographs of teenage girls, imagining they had run away and gathered together in solidarity along interstates and in forests, living in communal bliss. At the time, they were received under the umbrella of staged narrative photography but now are recognized for their feminist politics and homoerotic undercurrent.

12. Do you create with presentation in mind, be that a gallery show or a book?

> I make small work prints as I go, and I shuffle them around. This is the last time the process is private, and it's my greatest pleasure. I meet the challenges of exhibition and book separately, and with help from friends, editors, and gallerists. ❍

Kurland

"When a subject starts to keep me up at night, I know it will evolve into something larger."

Laub

Gillian Laub

First camera:
Polaroid OneStep from my grandpa
(the white one with a rainbow stripe
down the middle)

First meaningful photobook:
My mom's signed copy of Richard
Avedon's *Photographs 1947–1977* (1978).
I grew up with that on our coffee table.

Gillian Laub (born in Chappaqua, New York, 1975) is a
photographer and filmmaker based in New York. She received
a BA in comparative literature from the University of Wisconsin–
Madison before studying photography at the International Center
of Photography. Her works include the book *Testimony* (Aperture,
2007) and the book and film *Southern Rites* (2015).

First meaningful exhibition:
Roy DeCarava retrospective
at MoMA, in 1996

Personal fact:
When I was nine years old I secretly
got hooked on Dr. Ruth Westheimer's
Sunday night radio show, *Sexually
Speaking*. I used to call in on speed dial.
Once I got on the air and told her my
name was Sasha and made up a whole
story about catching my mom in bed
with my fiancé. In the middle of the
call my sister picked up the phone and
screamed, "Gillian get off the phone,
it's past your bedtime!"

1. What comes first for you: the idea for a project, or individual photographs that suggest a concept?

All my projects start with an idea, which is quickly followed by making my first images. The projects I work on all originate from a need to understand people or a place more deeply. I have spent the last two decades investigating political conflicts, exploring family and community relationships, and challenging assumptions about cultural identity. I tell stories utilizing different mediums—photography, oral history, text, and video. But the goal is always to uncover, and then communicate, some emotional truth.

When a subject starts to keep me up at night, I know it will evolve into something larger. At that point, the arc is very similar with most of my projects. Several weeks are spent focused on making photographs, interviewing, and filming, followed by many months in the editing room, studying and digesting the work. Once I have fully processed that material, I then go back to make more work. This process can go on for years—which is sometimes how long it takes to figure out the most effective way to build the narrative. One example of this is my project Southern Rites, which emerged over the course of twelve years spent getting to know the community of Montgomery County, Georgia. It started in 2002 as a commission by Spin magazine to photograph the local high school's racially segregated homecoming and prom rituals. I was so haunted by what I witnessed that I kept returning, hoping the exact shape of the project would reveal itself.

A few years later, in 2009, some of my photographs and audio interviews were published in the New York Times Magazine, bringing national attention to the town for the first time, and serving as the catalyst for the integration of the proms the following year. Yet I knew the proms were part of a larger story that I still hadn't managed to fully uncover. I kept photographing and began filming.

Then, in 2011, the murder of an unarmed young black man—whose family I had come to know over the years—by an older white man, seemed to confirm every assumption about the legacy of inequality and prejudice that the community was struggling to relinquish. A larger story needed to be told; so the project, which began as an exploration of segregated high school rituals, evolved into a decade-long mandate to confront painful, deeply rooted national realities in a feature-length documentary film, a book [published in 2015], and a traveling exhibition. I definitely did not see what it would turn into when I got that original commission, but that's how it often is with me: the subjects determine the shape of their own stories.

2. What are the key elements that must be present for you when you are creating a body of work? (Social commentary, strong form, personal connection, photographic reference…)

> The desire to tell stories, and the capacity for intimacy. I care about and make work that is itself social commentary. And I get very personal because the personal is always political and vice versa. My images become narratives that are always seeking a deeper understanding of the human condition, the family and tribe, in all its forms.

3. Is the idea of a body of work important to you? How does it function in relation to making a great individual photograph?

> Within every great body of work are successful individual photographs, but—yes—I'd say the body of work is the goal because it involves a development of thought, process, and action. That said, I do make many commissioned photographs, and there is something so satisfying—even joyful—about setting out to make one great image that reveals a whole narrative. This also can often lead to the unfolding of something larger. The key for me is to feel satisfied by the story that is ultimately told.

4. Do you have what you might call a "photographic style"?

> If I had to describe my photographic style it would be a mix of a documentary approach and a portraiture practice. But I don't like getting caught up or married to any particular "style." I am more preoccupied with subject matter and the transmission of emotional or political realities.

5. Where would you say your style falls on a continuum between completely intuitive and intellectually formulated?

> My intuition and my heart certainly lead my intellect. In fact, at this point I believe my gut is my intellect.

Laub

6. Assuming you now shoot in what you would consider your natural voice, have you ever wished your voice was different?

> I believe it's important to stay true to your voice, but to continue to evolve. It's always important to check in on how you are expressing yourself, to avoid getting too comfortable, and to be experimental. I never want to keep making the same photo over and over again.

7. How do you know when a body of work is finished?

> Somewhat maddeningly, I never feel finished. Each project is different. I thought the work for *Testimony* [portraits of Israeli Jews, Israeli Arabs, displaced Lebanese families, and Palestinians; 2007] would just be made during the Second Intifada, until I realized it was important to continue to work during the Israeli war with Lebanon in 2006. But honestly, I could've continued to make that work for many years after.

8. Have you ever had a body of work that was created in the editing process?

> Not as of yet. I am always pretty aware of what comprises the body of work before the editing process begins, and each has several different iterations of editing. All my work is very intentional. I have, though, discovered unexpected themes and patterns while I am editing.

9. Do you associate your work with a particular genre of photography? If yes, how would you define that genre?

> The word *genre* scares me because I don't like to be pigeonholed into any box or title, but I do consider myself a concerned photographer. I am never a fly on the wall. My process is very interactive, and I am very influenced by documentary and portrait narrative work. I strive for visual activism.

10. Do you ever revisit a series that has already been exhibited or published to shoot more and add to it?

> Yes, often. I feel like *Testimony* never ended, even though the book was published eleven years ago. I still make photographs that I consider part of that work. The dialogue and discovery still continue for me.

11. Do you ever revisit a series that has already been exhibited or published and *reedit* it?

> Yes, I love seeing older work with new eyes and perspective. *Southern Rites* has now been expanded into a traveling museum show, so I recently reinterviewed everyone photographed and have updated each caption with contemporary quotes. I am now showing a new edit with some unpublished images. They seem more relevant as time has passed. Also, I have been photographing my own family for almost twenty years. The work has been only exhibited once, and I wish I could go back and reedit that exhibition. In hindsight, I am not happy with what was shown. There is a reason why I have waited twenty years to make a final edit.

12. Do you create with presentation in mind, be that a gallery show or a book?

> I never know the final form when I'm beginning, or am in the middle of, creating work. It seems counterintuitive to me and my process and too formulaic. So much about the work is what I discover during the process. ◑

Laub

"I'm often thinking about the printed object when I'm photographing, and the act of printing has often suggested possibilities for new photographs."

John Lehr

First camera:
Kodak Instamatic 110

First meaningful photobook:
The Americans (1958) by
Robert Frank

Lehr

John Lehr (born in Baltimore, 1975) received a BFA from the
Maryland Institute College of Art in 1998 and an MFA from Yale
University School of Art in 2005. He is an associate professor of
photography at Pratt Institute. *The Island Position* (2019) is his
debut monograph. He lives in Philadelphia.

First meaningful exhibition:
*Pleasures and Terrors of Domestic
Comfort*, Baltimore Museum
of Art, 1992

Personal fact:
I learned how to perform magic from
my father, and worked as a professional
magician from the age of eight until I
was seventeen.

1. What comes first for you: the idea for a project, or individual photographs that suggest a concept?

> Individual photographs come first. I never know what I'm going to photograph when I set out in the morning. I think the pictures often begin with something that puzzles me, or something I feel I have a certain affection for. The process of making the pictures is how I figure out where that's coming from.

> For me what has worked is creating a space for surprise. This means that I have to be out in the world in a very open frame of mind where I'm not looking for anything in particular but I'm somehow sensitive to everything.

> I can't sit in a room without any stimuli and articulate what it is that I *mean*. One of the reasons I'm drawn to photography is because it's a medium where you can go out and make a picture and when you come back to the studio and look at it, you say, "Oh right, *that* is what I'm interested in, *that's* what I mean." You're able to collaborate with the swirling, disjointed world of experience and make a picture that retains some of that chaos alongside an unmistakable sense of authorship.

> Having said all this, I really believe there is also a place in between the two options in the question. Each of us carries around with us a set of interests about ourselves, about the world, and that guides everything we do when we photograph.

2. What are the key elements that must be present for you when you are creating a body of work? (Social commentary, strong form, personal connection, photographic reference…)

> The work always begins with oneself. That's the core, but I also want to address both the culture that I'm living in and photography itself. Those three things always have to be there.

> In my case, when I say photography, I mean the very particular possibilities —a certain kind of camera, a certain kind of film, and a certain kind of printing technology—it offers up. What are those possibilities, and how do they allow you to make different kinds of discoveries in the world?

3. Is the idea of a body of work important to you? How does it function in relation to making a great individual photograph?

> Yes. Photography is powerful as a serial medium. One of the things that I've seen and appreciated from the photographers that I admire is that the meaning, although it can be severely contained in a single picture, broadens and blossoms in a larger body of work.

4. Do you have what you might call a "photographic style"?

> I've spent very little time thinking about style and a great deal of time thinking about voice. I've worked to harness the visual equivalent of intonation, pitch, and articulation across bodies of work and within passages of individual pictures. None of these things are applied broadly or in a premeditated way. I do often limit the variables within a given project, but that is simply because I want to expand my awareness of new problems and possibilities.

5. Where would you say your style falls on a continuum between completely intuitive and intellectually formulated?

> I don't see these two as being opposed to one another. I do a lot of thinking, research, and preparation when I'm not photographing. This includes everything from reading and looking at art to analyzing my past successes and failures. All of this creates a kind of muscle memory that is present when I'm making my work. As I mentioned earlier, for me it's important to remain open when I'm photographing, but this openness is only productive when I've done the hard work of preparing my body and my mind to be receptive to a given slice of space and time.

6. Assuming you now shoot in what you would consider your natural voice, have you ever wished your voice was different?

> No. I realized early on that my work will always be at the service of my experience. If I've felt any frustration in this regard I think it has more to do with worrying that I'm unable to convey whatever it is I want to say.

7. How do you know when a body of work is finished?

> For me, it's finished when I feel like I have nothing more to add to what I've done or when I feel as though I'm beginning to repeat myself. This is really interesting for me right now because I'm working on a project called *The Island Position* [to be published in 2019] that contains the largest number of pictures I've ever made, and I don't feel like it's done. I still feel like I'm noticing new things. That's how I know it's not finished.

8. Have you ever had a body of work that was created in the editing process?

> Over the last ten years I've developed a way of working where I don't prioritize the experience of photographing over the printing process. I honestly don't even feel like one of these steps comes first, because I'm often thinking about the printed object when I'm photographing, and the act of printing has often suggested possibilities for new photographs.

9. Do you associate your work with a particular genre of photography? If yes, how would you define that genre?

> I'm uncomfortable with genre, and style too, because it suggests work can be roughly categorized by identifying simply how it looks or how it is like other things. It's much more difficult, and more pleasurable, to look and think deeply about work on its own terms. I do feel very connected to a certain way of working that fuses a deep interest in social issues with personal concerns, while also investigating the potentials of photography. I think of photography as a true medium, it's this thing that exists between me and the world, and it's what allows me to make certain kinds of discoveries. The materials I'm using are not simply in service to ideas that I have. The process and the materials can suggest something I'd never be able to imagine. If I had to map this out in a way that's reflected in my process it might go something like: Discovery > Accident > Surprise

10. Do you ever revisit a series that has already been exhibited or published to shoot more and add to it?

> Yes. I've always thought of an exhibition as just a glimpse into where an artist is at a particular time. I never think of exhibitions as either the beginning or the end.

11. Do you ever revisit a series that has already been exhibited or published and reedit it?

       Not to date.

12. Do you create with presentation in mind, be that a gallery show or a book?

       Some of my earliest experiences with photography were at museums, and so from an early age, I became really interested in how photographs can function in a physical space. Although there is this great tradition of photography and the book, I'm especially fascinated by the physicality and expressive possibilities of a picture in real space. I think we're still very much at the beginning of a time when artists are exploring the ways in which photographic objects can elicit an experience that can be felt in the body. ❍

Lehr

135

"Style mostly comes from how you perceive your environment and translate that to a photographic image; how you relate to and connect with your subject and what you decide to leave in or out of the frame."

Dana Lixenberg

First camera:
Nikon FM2, which I bought with
money I made from waitressing at
Caffé Dante in the Village when I
was eighteen, after working as an
au pair in New York for one year.
This also was the year I took my first
photography class at Parsons and fell
in love with the medium.

First meaningful photobook:
That must have been the Diane
Arbus Aperture monograph (1972)!

Dana Lixenberg (born in Amsterdam, 1964) studied photography
at the London College of Printing (1984–86) and Gerrit Rietveld
Academie, Amsterdam (1987–89). The series Imperial Courts
(1993–2015), her most extensive body of work to date, was
awarded the Deutsche Börse Photography Prize in 2017. Her
books include *united states* (2001), *Jeffersonville, Indiana* (2005),
The Last Days of Shishmaref (2008), *Set Amsterdam* (2011), *De
Burgemeester/The Mayor* (2011), *Imperial Courts, 1993–2015*
(2015), and *Tupac Biggie* (2018). She lives and works in New York
and Amsterdam.

First meaningful exhibition:
My elementary school was around
the corner from the Stedelijk
Museum, so from age four until
twelve, I spent many a lunch
hour with my mom there. Edward
Kienholz's life-size work *The Beanery*
[1965] was definitely one of the
highlights; an intriguingly creepy,
smelly, adult world. Also, my dad
was an artist and attending his
exhibitions was a big event. Being
very much attuned to his mood and
absorbing his tension, I was always
concerned about how many people
would show up.

1. What comes first for you: the idea for a project or individual photographs that suggest a concept?

> I don't necessarily start out with a larger concept; often my long-term projects come through editorial assignments and commissions. For example, with *Jeffersonville, Indiana* [2005], a series of portraits and landscapes of the town's homeless population, I first went for *Jane* magazine and something just really struck me. I knew I had to go back, which I did over the course of seven years. I felt the subject matter deserved more attention—and to be shown in a context other than an editorial context. *The Last Days of Shishmaref* [2008], a project about a small island threatened by rising water levels, came about because I was invited by a documentary filmmaker. *Imperial Courts, 1993–2015* [2015], an extensive portrait of a community in Watts, Los Angeles, started with a story for a Dutch weekly magazine on the rebuilding of South-Central LA after the riots in 1992. During a subsequent visit, I secured an introduction to gang leader Tony Bogard, who led me to his community Imperial Courts, although I didn't actually start shooting until I was able to go back due to a grant I received in 1993. Ultimately it turned into a twenty-two-year project.

> I read up, and I prepare; I think about the subject matter, but there's no way I can know what to expect beforehand. Once I'm in a place, I start to make choices about how to approach it: what to show or not show. But I don't start out with a clear-cut idea.

2. What are the key elements that must be present for you when you are creating a body of work? (social commentary, strong form, personal connection, photographic reference ...)

> I like making something visible that's not immediately visible. And I like going to small environments that are contained and have clearly defined parameters I can explore within. There are certain issues that I'm interested in, which usually come from a place of social engagement.

> How I get to a topic or a place is often circumstantial. Once I'm there, it's like slowly peeling back the layers of an onion. You meet people, get to know their stories, you explore an environment—and then it slowly becomes concrete; I start to dig deeper, and a personal connection develops. I get to that place just by being present and having my sensors open and letting go of my preconceptions. And then very quickly I have to shift into a higher gear and start making decisions about how to

move forward with the project. Working with a large-format camera is a big part of this. You engage with people in a certain way that becomes very focused. We're both in a vulnerable spot. The subject more so, of course, but I also have to really open myself, which can be daunting. It's emotionally challenging to get myself into that mindset. There's something quite beautiful and magical about this exchange with another person.

3. Is the idea of a body of work important to you? How does it function in relation to making a great individual photograph?

For me, it's important that a body of work consist of individually strong photographs. That each piece in a series can tell its own unique story, that it can be read by itself, even though the broader context is provided by its grouping with the other works in the series.

4. Do you have something you might call "a photographic style"?

I guess so, even if I'm not consciously aware of it. People will mention that they recognize my work, the way I photograph people. This was especially true when I was doing a lot of editorial work and had an immediate public platform, from the mid-1990s until the mid-2000s. All my work since 1993 has been done with a large-format 4-by-5-inch field camera, always with the same standard lens. Working with this camera, from a tripod, lends a sense of formality to a shoot, and a rigorous focus on details and composition. But style mostly comes from how you perceive your environment and translate that to a photographic image; how you relate to and connect with your subject and decide what to leave in or out of the frame.

5. Where would you say your photographic style falls on a continuum between completely intuitive and an intellectually formulated construct?

I would call myself an intuitive photographer, not a conceptual one. Ultimately a new project will only really start to take shape once I jump into the deep and start shooting. But that intuition is of course shaped and influenced by the knowledge I've gained about the broader context of the subject, specific research I've done, my understanding of photo and art history, and personal experience. All this informs the choices I make in terms of subject matter and approach.

6. Assuming you now shoot in what you would consider your natural voice, do you ever, or have you ever, hoped your voice was different?

> Only that my voice could be served by a camera that I could slide into my pocket, instead of having to schlep such a cumbersome camera, not to mention the tripod, cassettes, film, and lighting! Sometimes I feel a little restricted by process, even though I have a relatively compact set-up at this point. You often have to crawl on your knees to compose an image. And now I have to focus through my reading glasses. As you get older it gets more challenging. But for my purposes, I've not found a better tool. I love my Wista camera. It has become an extension of myself. You can't just bang the photographs out; each frame matters. It requires a lot of concentration, from both sides of the camera. In this quiet process, I try to bring the person to a place where they let go and they are not too consciously presenting a persona. It's always a delicate dance between the subject and myself.

7. How do you know when a body of work is finished?

> When I've reached a saturation point! It's a bit intuitive. It can come when the work starts to feel like I'm just producing more of the same. With some projects there's a specific deadline/time frame. But the ideal scenario is when the project is open-ended and it comes to an organic finish, like with *Imperial Courts*. I started working toward a first comprehensive presentation of the project as a book and an exhibition when the third generation of people I had been photographing was born—and the community had been waiting long enough for the book.

> I usually have a slightly unfinished feeling when I'm working on something. I'm always consumed by doubt.

8. Have you ever had a body of work that was created in the editing process?

> My first museum show in the Netherlands was a specific selection of works produced through editorial assignments that I grouped together under the title *united states* [published in 2001]. Thus a concept was forged in the editing process. It's the same with my last show at GRIMM, my gallery in Amsterdam. *American Images* contained a selection of portraits of American cultural icons mostly from the '90s, including the deceased rappers Christopher Wallace (aka Biggie Smalls) and Tupac Shakur. That show will come to GRIMM's New York space, and the edit will change again; I take my time and keep looking back at my archive.

Because I do all my work with the same camera, I feel it can all live together in some way. You can reshuffle it and look at it in different ways over time.

9. Do you associate your work with a particular genre of photography? If yes, how would you define that genre?

I consider myself a documentary photographer, which I think of as a very inclusive genre. I've moved between different contexts and I feel I've grown as an artist thanks to my extensive editorial practice. But all my work is rooted in and a response to the world as I find it: reality, no matter how surreal. Of course, *reality* is a complicated term. Fiction can, at times, be a better form to convey the real world.

As a portraitist, I feel that the portraits should work separately from the context of the larger stories or issues I'm addressing. When I'm photographing someone, I'm not thinking, "This person can illustrate this issue." I'm trying to make a study of that individual. My interest in the person really comes together in a visual way in the moment I'm in front of them, looking at them with clarity, usually from a place of great affection or at least from a place of respect.

10. Do you ever revisit a series that has already been exhibited or published to shoot more and add to it?

Yes, I've done this with the *Jeffersonville, Indiana* project. The book and exhibition were presented in 2005, and in 2013 I decided on a return visit. With the support of *TIME LightBox*, I produced some new portraits. And now I'm playing with the idea of going back again, maybe for a more extensive period.

More significantly, I've done this with *Imperial Courts*. I produced the first series of portraits in 1993. The work was presented in an exhibition that same year, and *Vibe* published a portfolio of the work. Then it disappeared in a drawer. I stayed in touch with the community, but it took me fifteen years to revisit it with my camera, after which I continued for eight consecutive years before I presented the project in book form and as a comprehensive exhibition, which included prints, a three-channel video installation, and a soundscape. And as life in the community continues, a community I've become emotionally invested in and visit on a regular basis, I consider it quite likely that at some point I will proceed to make new work in Imperial Courts.

11. Do you ever revisit a series that has already been exhibited or published and *reedit* it?

> So far, no, though in the case of *Imperial Courts*, due to the quantity of works (there are around three hundred photographs), I've made a different selection for each exhibition, dictated by the size and layout of the different spaces and taking the local cultural context into consideration. I doubt I would ever reedit the book with the work I've done to date, however.

12. Do you create with presentation in mind, be that gallery show or book?

> When working on a project, I always work toward a publication. I've presented all my completed projects in book form. For me, it's a very exciting and at times unnerving process to edit the work, and collaborate with a talented designer and bounce ideas back and forth, sometimes seemingly endlessly, to decide what form it needs to have, until we've created an object that is a work by itself, complete but never perfect. A book can travel more easily around the world than an exhibition and can be privately interacted with or consumed.

> Each of my projects thus far has led to making an exhibition as well. Of course, there's a very different editing process involved, equally interesting and challenging. I tend to select the works with the space of the exhibition in mind. Due to their rich texture and quality, as well as different sizes, photographic prints can make for a more detailed and visceral read than when the same images are reproduced in a book.

> Sometimes it's good not to rush toward a specific outcome or deadline for a body of work, to let the passage of time be a factor and to just see where it goes. ❶

Andrew Moore

First camera:
I purchased a plastic 35 mm Ansco camera with three books of S&H Green Stamps that I had carefully pasted together over several months. (There's an Andy Warhol silk-screen painting of those iconic stamps that is one of my favorites of his work.)

First meaningful photobook:
Clarence John Laughlin: The Personal Eye (1973)

Andrew Moore (born in Old Greenwich, Connecticut, 1957) is a recipient of a Guggenheim Fellowship and New York State Council on the Arts grant, among other awards. Moore's publications include *Inside Havana* (2002), *Governors Island* (with Lisa Kereszi, 2004), *Russia* (2005), *Detroit Disassembled* (2010), *Making History* (2010), *Cuba* (2012), *Dirt Meridian* (2015), and *Blue Alabama* (forthcoming in 2019). He lectured for ten years at Princeton University and has taught photography at the School of Visual Arts since 2004.

Moore

First meaningful exhibition:
The first exhibition I remember being impressed by was a retrospective of Andrew Wyeth at the Pennsylvania Academy of the Fine Arts in Philadelphia in either 1966 or 1967.

Personal fact:
In the house I grew up in, there was a very narrow bathroom with enormous wall mirrors that faced one another. The mirrors created an endless replication of the room and the ceiling lamp, and I spent many hours staring, trying to see around myself and follow the repeated trail of light as it veered off into seeming infinity.

1. What comes first for you: the idea for a project, or individual photographs that suggest a concept?

> I begin with an intuition, an intangible feeling about a certain connectivity between a place and our moment in history. Then I start making pictures while looking for clues in the work to see if there are deeper threads to follow. Ultimately, the resulting concepts evolve through the work itself.

2. What are the key elements that must be present for you when you are creating a body of work? (Social commentary, strong form, personal connection, photographic reference ...)

> a) The ripeness of a place in a specific moment in time.
> b) Personal connections that grow and branch out over the course of the work.
> c) A subject that is seemingly unappealing but in fact is multifaceted.
> d) Picturemaking that demands new formulations and approaches.

3. Is the idea of a body of work important to you? How does it function in relation to making a great individual photograph?

> It's necessary in order to create a broad emotional spectrum as well as offer the viewer a sense of totality or completeness of vision. But within a body of work there must exist a few "great" pictures that can summarize the whole project.

4. Do you have what you might call a "photographic style"?

> My "style" has evolved over many years and is still a work in progress. But I would say my best pictures have some of the following elements:
>
> · A highly formal and geometrically complex arrangement across the picture plane. This includes an extreme awareness of the framing, as often I compose from the edges toward the interior.
>
> · A palette, arranged into sets and subsets, what might be called "color counterpoint." Color and emotion are indivisible in my work, and so the more successful the counterpoint, the greater the emotional range.
>
> · The "third thing." This is the most elusive and necessary quality for me. It is nearly impossible to quantify, but broadly defined, it is the element that acts as a catalyst on the rest of the image.

5. Where would you say your style falls on a continuum between completely intuitive and intellectually formulated?

> Although I photograph in all states of mind, my highest aspiration is this ideal: to get up on the razor's edge, to be in a place where I'm completely focused on a specific idea, and at the very same moment, can act spontaneously and incorporate new stimuli. That's the very fine point of balance, where one has the deep trust of their intuitions fully at hand, and at the same time, the total attentiveness that a living moment demands.

6. Assuming you now shoot in what you would consider your natural voice, have you ever wished your voice was different?

> No. My only ongoing wish is to remain flexible yet focused.

7. How do you know when a body of work is finished?

> A body of work has a natural progression over the years. The key period is when one has both the deep connection to the subject and the internal momentum of the work itself. Once the momentum has drained away, it's just a matter of finding a satisfying closure.

8. Have you ever had a body of work that was created in the editing process?

> No. I have had bodies of work brought to fulfillment by the edit but never made that way. What I do find useful these days is to edit (with outside help) when the work is nearly complete. This helps me look for holes in the overall design/image tapestry that I need to fill in going forward.

9. Do you associate your work with a particular genre of photography? If yes, how would you define that genre?

> I see my work as a hybrid of fine art, documentary, and journalism, in that I am blending both narrative and formal modes of picturemaking. In an art historical context, I see myself as a post-documentarian color photographer, bridging the gap between fact-oriented objective photography and more subjective and digitally processed image creation.

Moore

10. Do you ever revisit a series that has already been exhibited or published to shoot more and add to it?

> Only rarely, as "ripeness is all" in my subject matter. Times Square and Cuba [*Inside Havana*, 2002] are the only examples where I returned to a former subject with any degree of success.

11. Do you ever revisit a series that has already been exhibited or published and *reedit* it?

> No, with the exception of my book *Cuba* [2012] that is reedited with new photographs.

12. Do you create with presentation in mind, be that a gallery show or a book?

> Yes, absolutely. When I'm working, I am thinking both of large prints for exhibition as well as pictures to be sequenced in a book. The criteria can be very different, but I find this allows me to shoot a greater range of material. Some images are meant to be seen at scale, while others don't need scale but are essential to the overall flow of a publication. ◑

Abelardo Morell

First camera:
A family friend, someone I knew growing up in Cuba, gave me an old Contact camera—pretty primitive. I'm sure that it was obtained in a suspect way.

First meaningful photobook:
Henri Cartier-Bresson's
The Decisive Moment (1952)

Abelardo Morell (born in Havana, 1948) immigrated to the United States with his parents in 1962. He received a BA from Bowdoin College in 1977 and an MFA from the Yale University School of Art in 1981. His publications include *A Camera in a Room* (1995), a photographic illustration of *Alice's Adventures in Wonderland* (1998), *A Book of Books* (2002), *Camera Obscura* (2004), *Abelardo Morell* (2005), *The Universe Next Door* (2013), *Tent-Camera* (2018), and *Flowers for Lisa* (2018). Morell has received a number of awards and grants, including a Guggenheim Fellowship, International Center of Photography Infinity Award in Art, and Lucie Award for achievement in fine art. He lives in Newton, Massachusetts.

Morell

First meaningful exhibition:
MoMA's *Diane Arbus* (1972)

Personal fact:
In my early darkroom days, in 1969, I used to pick up other people's test strips and prints that they had put into the trash. I would then cut them up or pour darkroom chemicals over them, which would distort their appearance, and claim them as my own work.

1. What comes first for you: the idea for a project, or individual photographs that suggest a concept?

> Mostly, an idea comes to me first from a casual observation, a dream, or a mistake that points to something interesting. The real evolution comes from the making of the pictures and the testing of how reality shapes what I originally envisioned. However, the first mindful concept is super important because it involves a sort of primitive birth, even as we all know nobody is born perfect. I do like William Carlos Williams's dictum: "No ideas but in things."

2. What are the key elements that must be present for you when you are creating a body of work? (Social commentary, strong form, personal connection, photographic reference…)

> I do want everything I make to be beautiful in concept, shape, meaning, and the photographic quality of the print. I'm sure that, like most artists, most of what I make comes out of some undiscovered part of me. Certain shapes and motifs keep showing up in my pictures, and I'm not always sure why. For an artist it's probably best to not dig too much into that!
>
> Usually, I think that my need to create pictures has a lot to do with a desire to show an imaginary place that's made up with the stuff of reality—things that we all know and have names for. Ultimately, it's a way to share intimate parts of me. I don't intend my images to stand for anything political. While I realize and appreciate artists who do this very well, my inclination is not to have my images communicate in that realm.

3. Is the idea of a body of work important to you? How does it function in relation to making a great individual photograph?

> I have settled into working with coherent groups of images—I still want to make individually strong images, but I want them to exist in a group sharing similar themes. Declaring a subject helps me because I don't have to reinvent the wheel for each picture. I love the way jazz musicians often play standard songs everybody knows and it is within that framework that they bring all sorts of amazing invention to the song. Case in point is what John Coltrane did with "My Favorite Things."

4. Do you have what you might call a "photographic style"?

> One can't help producing things that have a personal stamp—we all have individual preferences and psychologies. We like what we like, and one's art tends to reflect that. But I think it's important to stray from your regular world sometimes and try new ways of picturing things and find new subjects to challenge you. In my own work, I have tried to make images of many different kinds of subjects like art history, books, and time of childhood, and I use a number of styles and processes for my projects, including Camera Obscura, Books, Still Life, Optics, Tent-Camera, Photograms, Cliché Verre, etc. Maybe it's my way of keeping my ego a bit off-balance and surprising myself in the process.

5. Where would you say your style falls on a continuum between completely intuitive and intellectually formulated?

> I hope right in the middle!

6. Assuming you now shoot in what you would consider your natural voice, have you ever wished your voice was different?

> Yes, one of the problems of finding a "voice" is that you then get stuck with it. Philip Glass talked about this in a 1999 interview with his cousin Ira Glass where he lamented that everything he writes sounds like Philip Glass. He went on to say: "I've always said to younger composers, it's not how do you find your voice but how to get rid of it. Getting the voice isn't hard, it's getting rid of the damn thing. Because once you've got the voice then you're kind of stuck with it." I do think that one is capable of containing a great variety of voices inside but often we settle into a reduced official persona. Some painters, in an attempt to break a pattern, begin to paint with their left hand. Some artists try to get themselves out of the way, like John Cage when he used pure chance to compose music.

7. How do you know when a body of work is finished?

> Some bodies of work never end—I keep finding interesting new ways to make Camera Obscura and Tent-Camera pictures. In the case of my latest project, *Flowers for Lisa*, which is now a book [2018], I think that I'm pretty much all done with it. I worked at a rather frenetic pace and it's good to put that to bed. But I bet you that flowers will bloom again in my imagination.

8. Have you ever had a body of work that was created in the editing process?

No.

9. Do you associate your work with a particular genre of photography? If yes, how would you define that genre?

Labels can be useful, but they can also be very confusing and damaging. In some ways, a good picture is a good picture no matter what camp it comes from. I like to think that what I make is art! In the continuum and trajectory of Albrecht Dürer, Francisco Goya, Paula Modersohn-Becker, Édouard Manet, Irving Penn, Agnes Martin, Manuel Álvares Bravo, Joan Mitchell . . . Art is a great house that covers a great variety of expressions—all of them stemming, at bottom, from an individual desire to make sense.

10. Do you ever revisit a series that has already been exhibited or published to shoot more and add to it?

Yes, like in the case of the Camera Obscura imagery.

11. Do you ever revisit a series that has already been exhibited or published and *reedit* it?

I look (not often) at earlier work, and it's instructive to see what my youthful self liked and suffered from. I'm in the process of scanning early negatives, and it would be really interesting for my present self to edit some meaning and sense out of those works.

12. Do you create with presentation in mind, be that a gallery show or a book?

Yes, without a show or a book it's like the sound-of-a-tree-falling-in-the-forest quandary. Lately, I am more interested in shaping talks/lectures about my work. In these I include many, many art references. I find that paintings, prints, drawings, sculptures, movies, jokes all have a great deal of influence on what I make. ◑

Zora
Murff

First camera:
Nikon D3100 purchased for a course
I took at a community college

First meaningful photobook:
Daniel Shea's *Blisner, IL* (2014). It
was the first time that I really paid
attention to the narrative structure
in a photobook as well as the idea
of a photobook as an art object.

Zora Murff (born in Des Moines, Iowa, 1987) is an assistant
professor of photography at the University of Arkansas,
Fayetteville. He received a BS in psychology from Iowa State
University and an MFA in studio art from the University of
Nebraska, Lincoln. Murff was named an Aperture Portfolio Prize
finalist, a PDN 30 Honoree, and a Light Work artist-in-residence,
all in in 2019. Monographs of his work include *Corrections* (2015),
Lost, Omaha (2018), and *At No Point In Between* (2019).

First meaningful exhibition:
A permanent collections exhibition
at the Des Moines Art Center. I saw
Sally Mann's portrait *Emmet, Jessie,
and Virginia* (1989), and it was the
first time that a photograph made
me think of something other than
what was in the frame.

Personal fact:
I once met Dave Matthews in the
Lincoln, Nebraska, airport. He sat
down next to me, and I had to google
him because I thought he might have
been the actor Jeffrey Dean Morgan.
I introduced myself by asking him if
he was in fact Dave Matthews.

1. What comes first for you: the idea for a project, or individual photographs that suggest a concept?

    The idea. I'm not a prolific maker and I do a lot of reading, research, and reflection before embarking on a new project. Ideas get spread out between my notebooks, scraps of paper, in my phone. Once I feel I'm ready to start making images again, I'll consult those ideas and either recreate them or keep my eyes open while I'm out photographing.

2. What are the key elements that must be present for you when you are creating a body of work? (Social commentary, strong form, personal connection, photographic reference...)

    When I was studying psychology, on the first day of a counseling methods course, the instructor said, "Before you can help anyone with their problems, you have to figure your own shit out." My approach to project-making is inward, then outward. Projects start with a series of questions about something, and I use photography as a means to work toward those answers. Once I feel I have a handle on my personal stake in the work, I begin making outward connections. Recently, I've been thinking a lot about contradictions present in my work. I was listening to a podcast about how scientific racism is embedded into current immigration policies. Liberal rhetoric is often used to decry xenophobia. But to work toward reconciliation, we have to take a hard look in the mirror and become accountable for our past. Things like the Black Lives Matter and Me Too movements weren't born from blindness toward self-criticism. What I'm trying to get at is that what is happening around you has a strong influence over what you have a desire to make.

3. Is the idea of a body of work important to you? How does it function in relation to making a great individual photograph?

    It is, and it isn't. A body of work is an interesting vehicle that I feel photography is in the midst of working out. I also think that the rapid growth of photobook publishing—both as a vehicle to make work and as an accomplishment—engenders feelings that it is a rule of photography. But I'm interested in what the next way of working might be. In relation to making a great individual photograph, I suppose that depends on how someone works. For me, I evaluate images individually to continually challenge myself to elevate the work that I make, whether I'm in the midst of making a body of work or making an image just because.

4. Do you have something you might call "a photographic style"?

> I do, but I haven't defined it yet. My wife and fellow artist, Rana Young, calls it "Neo-Documentary."

5. Where would you say your style falls on a continuum between completely intuitive and intellectually formulated?

> Intuitive formulations, maybe? I know what I want to make, but have to contend with the realities of actually making the damn thing. Staying open to the world is important. I'm also really deliberate and sometimes make the same version of an image a multitude of times until I feel that I finally have it right (or realize that the first version was the best).

6. Assuming you now shoot in what you would consider your natural voice, have you ever wished your voice was different?

> All the time. There's a lot of impactful work out there, a lot of artists that I admire. But my voice is always going to be my voice. I feel that this is another way to grow as an artist—not to copy other people's work—but to find inspiration and use it as a tool to challenge yourself to make something new and surprising.

7. How do you know when a body of work is finished?

> Both *Corrections* [published in 2015] and *At No Point In Between* [2019] were made over about three years, including the time that was devoted purely to answering research questions. However, both were attached to my studies, so there were natural wrap-up dates.

8. Have you ever had a body of work that was created in the editing process?

> The collaboration that I made with Rana was made in the editing process. We had a collection of what we called "orphan" images, photographs that we weren't using for anything. We decided to bring them together as a way to try out a collaboration, resulting in our ongoing project Fade Like a Sigh.

Murff

9. Do you associate your work with a particular genre of photography? If yes, how would you define that genre?

> Definitely with documentary photography. My early mentors were very strong documentarians, so it only makes sense that when I first began studying photography, I had a heavy interest in that genre. I would define it as the movement to use photography as an objective document; to record and provide commentary on both the extraordinary and the quotidian. I'm a realist in a lot of ways, but I enjoy emphasizing the photograph's failure to convey "truth." That gray area fascinates me.

10. Do you ever revisit a series that has already been exhibited or published to shoot more and add to it?

> In fact, just this past weekend was the first time that I've added to an existing body of work. I decided to make a short film to help round out At No Point In Between conceptually. So yes.

11. Do you ever revisit a series that has already been exhibited or published and *reedit* it?

> Definitely. One of the beautiful things about what artists do is that we continually educate ourselves about what we make. We have multiple opportunities to do this through publishing, lecturing, exhibiting, etc. I like to use those opportunities to reframe/reposition my work because I do, of course, change, or can find something else that also makes sense in relation to the work. Why does the body of work have to be static?

12. Do you create with presentation in mind, be that a gallery show or a book?

> With my first body of work, *Corrections*, I didn't have any clear intention for how the work would exist once it was finished. With my second body of work, *At No Point In Between*, I knew that I wanted it to be a book from the beginning. While that choice didn't sway how I thought about the work conceptually, it skewed how I sequenced or curated the images: I was always thinking about those facing pages. ◑

Catherine Opie

Catherine Opie (born in Sandusky, Ohio, 1961) received a BFA from the San Francisco Art Institute in 1985 and an MFA from the California Institute of the Arts in 1988. She was awarded a 2019 Guggenheim Fellowship, the Smithsonian's Archives of American Art Medal in 2016, the Julius Shulman Excellence in Photography Award, and a United States Artists Fellowship, among other honors. Opie has published nearly a dozen books, including *In and Around the Home* (2006), *Empty and Full* (2011), *700 Nimes Road* (2015), and *Keeping an Eye on the World* (2017). She has been a professor of photography at the University of California, Los Angeles, since 2001.

Opie

1. What comes first for you: the idea for a project, or individual photographs that suggest a concept?

   Normally the idea of the project comes first. When I begin to make a body of work, surprises or different situations often happen that allow me to think within the original idea but still experiment. So I like to start with a concept, but I also like the freedom of how it can transpire during the making of the work.

2. What are the key elements that must be present for you when you are creating a body of work? (Social commentary, strong form, personal connection, photographic reference...)

   All of the above. It's important that my photographs have the ability to tell stories. I'm also very formally concerned when I make images. If I were to write a recipe for my photographs, it would be a combo of light, thought, and the ability to carry forth a dialogue in relationship to what an image represents in history.

3. Is the idea of a body of work important to you? How does it function in relation to making a great individual photograph?

   Most artists during the '80s in art school were trained to make bodies of work. Individual photos obviously stand out in bodies of work, but I'm most interested in the ideas around how an exhibition is created or how multiple photographs begin to create a narrative.

4. Do you have what you might call a "photographic style"?

   People are often confused—they think that I don't have a photographic style because of the diversity of images that I make, but I feel there is a stylistic formality embedded in my various bodies of work.

5. Where would you say your style falls on a continuum between completely intuitive and intellectually formulated?

   I was very formally trained—I graduated with my BA and MFA from art schools with very distinguished professors [San Francisco Art Institute and CalArts] and have studied photography my entire life. After that kind of education, I can't say that it comes from an intuitive place.

6. Assuming you now shoot in what you would consider your natural voice, have you ever wished your voice was different?

> It depends on what you think of as a natural voice. We all go to this kind of comfort zone when making work, but I always feel it's more important to break through those zones to move forward and try to make something that's challenging in conceiving a different body of work.

7. How do you know when a body of work is finished?

> Sometimes I don't know. Sometimes there's a natural end point due to circumstances. And there are times you want a body of work to last forever but then it ends up finishing because of exhibitions. There also are open-ended projects, such as Political Landscapes [2006–ongoing] or Portraits [2012–ongoing].

8. Have you ever had a body of work that was created in the editing process?

> Yes, my recent film *The Modernist* [2017] had to be heavily edited. The finished film contains eight hundred photographs and ended up being twenty-two minutes of a series of still images.

> Photography is always edited. I think most photographers look at contact sheets and begin to formulate their ideas. Their ability to make many images is different from other mediums. Photographers can very quickly make an enormous amount of images that then need to be edited.

9. Do you associate your work with a particular genre of photography? If yes, how would you define that genre?

> In the beginning of making photographs I decided that I needed to define myself within a genre: I would often call myself a social documentary photographer. Ultimately, I realized that I'm interested in ideas around democracy and humanity and the ability for the camera to record these ideas in relation to history.

10. Do you ever revisit a series that has already been exhibited or published to shoot more and add to it?

> No. But I do have open-ended series that have been exhibited that I'm still working on.

Opie

11. Do you ever revisit a series that has already been exhibited or published and reedit it?

No.

12. Do you create with presentation in mind, be that a gallery show or a book?

Absolutely. Photography is not a single image that hangs on a wall, it has to work spatially in relationship to the design of an exhibition. Sequencing, form, and shape are all inherent within the way I begin to conceive an exhibition. ◑

Opie

Ed
Panar

First camera:
Kodak Instamatic 110

First meaningful photobook:
I saw Wolfgang Tillmans's *Burg* (1998), thanks to Chris McCall from Pier 24 Photography, whom I went to undergrad with; I bought Nick Waplington's *Safety in Numbers* (2000).

Ed Panar (born in Johnstown, Pennsylvania, 1976) holds a BA from Indiana University of Pennsylvania (1998) and an MFA from Cranbrook Academy of Art, Bloomfield Hills, Michigan (2005). He has been a visiting faculty member at numerous institutions, including Image Text Ithaca. Among his publications are *Golden Palms* (2007), *Same Difference* (2010), *Animals That Saw Me* (2011), *Salad Days* (2011), *Nothing Changes If Nothing Changes* (2013), *April Flowers* (2015), *Falling Asleep* (2015), *Animals That Saw Me: Volume Two* (2016), and *In the Vicinity* (2018). He is based in Pittsburgh.

Panar

Personal fact:
I shot my first roll of film during a fifth-grade field trip. My best friend and I had our own detective agency and used a camera to document our investigations. My involvement with print media began in the late 1980s, when, at the age of thirteen, I became a newspaper carrier for Johnstown, Pennsylvania's *Tribune-Democrat*.

1. What comes first for you: the idea for a project, or individual photographs that suggest a concept?

> It usually consists of some combination of the two. I find that the photographs themselves lead the way or foreshadow future projects, but it often takes some other type of insight, inspiration, or amount of time passing for their potential to be made apparent. My favorite moments are when I am inspired with what feels like a new idea or concept, only to discover that I had already been working on it photographically.

2. What are the key elements that must be present for you when you are creating a body of work? (Social commentary, strong form, personal connection, photographic reference ...)

> A sense of a new suggestion. An intuitive "form," which, for me, is the feeling that there are hidden threads that I may not fully understand but are undeniably present. A sense of specificity, even when the aim is openness and ambiguity. Something new and unexpected, even if it is so subtle you could miss it at first glance.

3. Is the idea of a body of work important to you? How does it function in relation to making a great individual photograph?

> It is intrinsic for me. Individual photographs, when shown together, always imply a body of work, otherwise why bring them together? I am most interested in how photographs operate when placed in relation to others, but each photograph needs to be able to stand on its own as well as meet the needs of the project at hand. The challenge and joy of striving to make better photographs is a never-ending game.

4. Do you have what you might call a "photographic style"?

> I don't really think of it in that way. Is taking photographs in a primarily clear and direct fashion a style? If so, it is a style that is about looking and drawing from the world material and meaning, and allowing for a certain level of openness and questioning. This almost seems to imply a type of nonstyle or antistyle.

5. Where would you say your style falls on a continuum between completely intuitive and intellectually formulated?

> I would like to think of my way of working as somewhere between the two, or better yet, where the two modes mix. I don't think they have to be mutually exclusive.

6. Assuming you now shoot in what you would consider your natural voice, have you ever wished your voice was different?

> I don't want to keep the same voice forever, but I also don't want to feel like the "voice" is the only important feature. Hopefully the subject matter can have a place at the table. I'm always trying to subtly shift the voice in my pictures to the things being depicted, and not just my observation of them. It might be a paradoxical approach, but photography seems to be okay with paradoxes.

7. How do you know when a body of work is finished?

> When it feels like there's nothing left to add, or there's no further territory worth exploring, which usually coincides with a drop-off of interest and excitement. Unfortunately, there is often still quite a bit of work to be done to truly finish a project at this point, which is good to remember. Some projects are self-contained by a parameter such as a period of time, a particular place, or an event. A project feels most finished when it preserves the idea from that moment in a satisfactory way, and also has taken on a form that I can revisit in the future.

8. Have you ever had a body of work that was created in the editing process?

> Absolutely. For me the edit becomes the work, which is why it can be so difficult to pull it aside and look at it separately. It's also important to note that many projects allow for multiple edits. The specific edit chosen for a book project, for example, should stand on its own in order to function most effectively as a book, but this doesn't mean that other edits from the same body of work might not also exist.

Panar

9. Do you associate your work with a particular genre of photography? If yes, how would you define that genre?

> I don't really think of myself as working within a genre, but I do feel like my work could be viewed as part of a way of working in photography historically. The mode that Walker Evans called "documentary style" comes to mind.

10. Do you ever revisit a series that has already been exhibited or published to shoot more and add to it?

> Absolutely. For me, many of my projects are ongoing and long-term. I'm interested in how time can "change" photographs, so sometimes it literally takes years to get to the point where I find the right place for certain images. I don't think it's a coincidence that many photography projects are seen differently after time has passed, and maybe that's why there's a lot of effort spent in the photo world looking back at older things, seeing how perceptions have changed, how we've changed, noticing things differently. This is one of my favorite parts of photography, the fact that as static as images might appear, they don't really stay the same.

11. Do you ever revisit a series that has already been exhibited or published and *reedit* it?

> Again, absolutely. Although there are some works that I consider final, such as published book edits, most of my projects extend beyond a specific edit or iteration as most presentations do not allow for a complete series to be viewed all at once. Trying to understand the edges of a project, and defining what essential parameters are necessary for it to become its own thing—and how that can be translated and communicated through a specific form—is the name of the game.

12. Do you create with presentation in mind, be that a gallery show or a book?

> Not really. For me, the final form or presentation comes from the activity of gathering things that may not have had anything to do with one another when they were made. When I am out shooting I try to make photographs in as open a way as possible. That means seeking out pictures that have the ability to surprise me, ones that I can't quite understand entirely, and hopefully will lead to some new area of discovery.

I've always been fascinated by the "happy accident" and the unplanned coincidence, so I try to create circumstances in both the shooting and editing processes where those things might more likely occur. Part of that has been building an archive, which over time allows for working from layers and layers of pictures. Planting enough seeds and tending to the garden can inspire connections and sparks that you couldn't have imagined at the beginning, and that is when editing starts to get interesting. ◑

Panar

"I find it best to remain responsive to what is going on in front of my camera rather than be concerned with whether what I'm doing will work in the context of other pictures."

Matthew Pillsbury

First camera:
I used my dad's old Yashica in high school, but my first camera was a basic Nikon 35 mm, all manual. It was stolen from me while I was walking down the street, the week after I got my first 8-by-10 camera.

First meaningful photobook:
In high school my parents gave me the multivolume *The Work of Atget* (edited by John Szarkowski and Maria Morris Hambourg, 1981).

American photographer **Matthew Pillsbury** (born in Neuilly, France, 1973) lives and works in New York. He has a BA in fine arts from Yale University (1995) and an MFA from the School of Visual Arts (2004), and has been a recipient of a Guggenheim Fellowship and the HSBC award. Pillsbury is the author of *Time Frame* (2007) and *City Stages* (Aperture, 2013).

First meaningful exhibition:
New Photography at MoMA, in 1994, where I discovered the work of Abelardo Morell.

Personal fact:
In my one-and-done acting career, I played the illegitimate child of Catherine Deneuve and Jean-Louis Trintignant's characters in *Le Bon Plaisir* (directed by Francis Girod, 1984).

1. What comes first for you: the idea for a project, or individual photographs that suggest a concept?

   > I've never conceived of a body of work before making it. I'm always photographing, and I let the images guide me. The only exception is when I've decided to focus on a specific city, but even then I remain open to what I actually photograph and the images build upon themselves. While I have to plan some of the locations, I wouldn't say that there is an idea for the group of images as much as there is the desire to explore a given place.

2. What are the key elements that must be present for you when you are creating a body of work? (Social commentary, strong form, personal connection, photographic reference…)

   > The only thing that has to be there is a desire to make a photograph of whatever it is I'm looking at, in that moment. This will come out of a strong reaction to something beautiful in the world and wanting to make a picture that conveys the emotion I'm having. As I make the work, I think it's important to research past images that have been made in the same location or have addressed the same questions, but that's still not as crucial as that "in the moment" reaction.

3. Is the idea of a body of work important to you? How does it function in relation to making a great individual photograph?

   > It's secondary to making a great individual image, though obviously I hope for my images to come together and make some sense as a group. But they are each conceived individually, and I definitely have some images that exist on their own. Sometimes, their place in the larger body of work becomes more apparent over time, and sometimes they remain stand-alone images.

4. Do you have what you might call a "photographic style"?

   > Yes—all my work for the past fifteen years has been made using long exposures and available light. Even as I switched from working only in black and white to working predominantly in color, my style has remained consistent.

5. Where would you say your style falls on a continuum between completely intuitive and intellectually formulated?

> My first series, Screen Lives, started off as an intellectually formulated construct inspired by the [Hiroshi] Sugimoto movie theaters [in which an entire movie is captured in one long exposure]. In my case, each exposure was exactly the length of the TV show being watched. Over time, this approach has become completely intuitive.

6. Assuming you now shoot in what you would consider your natural voice, have you ever wished your voice was different?

> Yes. I spent my twenties making landscape photographs. Then, when I started graduate school I wanted to take pictures of my friends in their homes. Had I been able to light them properly and, perhaps more importantly, had I been comfortable directing them, I would have made more standard portraits. The use of available light and the long exposures were solutions to my technical and directorial failings. Ultimately, I was far more interested in the pictures that I made than the pictures I wanted to make. I think there's an important lesson there. In many ways the choice of equipment and working methodology is important inasmuch as you have to find the right tools to make the work that you want while also having a working process that you enjoy. Being miserable lighting and directing my friends never would have produced interesting images.

7. How do you know when a body of work is finished?

> I don't. As I said, I don't think of bodies of work. I would never not shoot a given scene just because I felt like I'd concluded that project.

8. Have you ever had a body of work that was created in the editing process?

> I think editing is always incredibly important. It was particularly challenging for *Sanctuary*, my last show at Benrubi Gallery [New York]. I wanted to mix serious political images with lighter scenes of people at play. Finding the balance of the two groups of images was hard and so was hanging images that were not immediately connected. The first sequences and edits we made were really awful and we worked for several months on which images to include and how to sequence them.

Pillsbury

I would say that the closest I have come to having a body of work made in editing was with my book *City Stages* [2013], which includes images that I made in New York, Paris, London, and other cities over a ten-year period. Working with my editor, we created a sequence and a body of work in its own right.

9. Do you associate your work with a particular genre of photography? If yes, how would you define that genre?

No. I really don't think of "genres of photography" much, in general. Many of my favorite photographers mix landscapes, portraits, and other kinds of images within the same project. In my twenties I made landscape photographs, and while my focus more recently has been on our urban lives I still find myself drawn to photographing in nature as well.

10. Do you ever revisit a series that has already been exhibited or published to shoot more and add to it?

Yes. I see myself making pictures that address the role of technology in our lives—the omnipresent screens of tablets, laptops, televisions, and phones—as an ongoing project. While I stopped focusing on the Screen Lives series in 2007 there have been more recent pictures that I consider part of the series, like the portrait *Fausto in Washington Square Park* [2011] or my self-portrait in Tokyo [2015]. So much has changed both in terms of the technology we use and the ways in which we use it that I feel ready to make more pictures to add to that series.

11. Do you ever revisit a series that has already been exhibited or published and *reedit* it?

Yes. Each time my work gets exhibited or when I work on a book I'll reedit and sequence the images. Every selection—whether it's a single print going into a group show, slides made for an application, or a full exhibition—is an opportunity to present my work and my ideas to a new audience.

One of my favorite experiences was looking back at the Screen Lives photographs and making an edit that focused on my romantic relationship with Nathan Noland. The exhibition *Nate and Me* in 2014 presented images that had been widely shown, but grouped them in a completely new way and in the process told a very different story. For the images of Nate and me, more often than not, I would set up the camera, but then we'd start watching television or checking our emails and totally forget the picture was being taken. Rather than a broader look at how we use technology in our lives the show became a very personal and autobiographical look at my life. Any interesting art is open to many interpretations, and by reediting a group of images I can put forth new ideas and new connections.

12. Do you create with presentation in mind, be that a gallery show or a book?

No. When I'm making a photograph I'm really only focused on the best way to capture what drew my eye. My preplanning efforts are often met with a different reality when in the moment of making the photograph. I find it best to remain responsive to what is going on in front of my camera rather than be concerned with whether what I'm doing will work in the context of other pictures. The only time that I have some concern for the presentation is while shooting on assignment, when I'm asked to do something specific, such as make a vertical picture, and find that a horizontal would work better. In that case, I will try to convince the editors to run the horizontal version instead. ◑

Pillsbury

"I'm interested in authenticity of voice. So, the more I trust myself, the more interested I become in my own ideas. The work begins to teach me about my own worldview."

Kristine Potter

First camera:
I remember asking my parents for a camera for my high school graduation, and I received a Canon Rebel X. I loved that camera and used it well into my first serious attempts at taking pictures.

First meaningful photobook:
In college I would spend much of my free time in the "TR" [photography] section of the library. I would create tall piles of books and sort through what I liked and disliked. The Diane Arbus monograph (Aperture, 1972) was easily the most fascinating book of the collection.

Kristine Potter (born in Dallas, 1977) is based in Nashville. She received a BFA and BA from the University of Georgia (2001) and an MFA from the Yale University School of Art (2005). Potter is a 2018 Guggenheim Fellow, and her first monograph, *Manifest*, was published in 2018.

First meaningful exhibition:
Around the age of twenty, I drove out to see the Rothko Chapel in Houston. Something about the duration of looking that the darkened chapel installation requires changed my perception of art forever.

Personal fact:
When it comes to motor skills, I'm cross-dominant, which means I favor different hands for different tasks. If it's a new task, or one I haven't practiced in a while, I have to try both hands to see which I can better control. Unfortunately, in baseball, I throw and catch left-handed, which essentially makes me a one-armed player. I was the last pick for every recess baseball game I can recall.

1. What comes first for you: the idea for a project, or individual photographs that suggest a concept?

> I would say it is probably an idea that is well informed by a history of photography (both my own and that of others). If we want to talk about long-term projects, I typically begin with a conceptual architecture that loosely defines where I'm going and whom I'm looking to find. When I first began work on *Manifest* [2018], for example, I thought it would be comprised entirely of portraits. But you'll notice that the body of work is full of landscape pictures: those evolved because the area, Colorado's Western Slope, was so sparsely populated that I would sometimes go a few days without making a portrait. There I was, in this incredible landscape that had all kinds of photographic history, holding a 4-by-5 camera. It came so naturally—and I can't imagine this work existing without the landscapes—but that wasn't the original plan. For me, it is increasingly important to avoid treating my initial concepts as a formula or something to illustrate. These ideas are necessarily loose and the magic usually happens at the margins.

2. What are the key elements that must be present for you when you are creating a body of work? (Social commentary, strong form, personal connection, photographic reference...)

> I simply have to be compelled to see it. Nothing is going to happen for me if I'm not deeply curious and driven to make the effort. I do find myself drawn to social issues as they relate to gender and gendered ways of seeing. I've thought a lot about why that might be true, and I can only figure that it has something to do with growing up in a military family with a bunch of brothers. Talk about fighting the patriarchy to get your voice heard!

3. Is the idea of a body of work important to you? How does it function in relation to making a great individual photograph?

> This is really a micro versus macro question. Arguably, a great individual photograph is always the endeavor. For me, it is the thrill of using the camera in the real world and trying to make all the elements work in a single instant. But context affects how that photograph works in the world, or for the viewer, and putting a box (even a nuanced one) around a group of photos gives them a way to influence and complicate one another. As with most things, I resist overexplaining my work. But saying that a group of pictures should be considered together says to the

viewer: "There is something happening in between these photos that is as important as what is happening in them. Do the work, and you will be rewarded."

4. Do you have what you might call a "photographic style"?

Oh, I'm sure that I do, but I doubt I'm the right person to name it.

5. Where would you say your style falls on a continuum between completely intuitive and intellectually formulated?

It is probably equally reliant on both modes of working. If I let one end of the spectrum have more influence, it is definitely the intuitive side. My instincts are generally more trustworthy than my rational thoughts.

6. Assuming you now shoot in what you would consider your natural voice, have you ever wished your voice was different?

Ha! I often wish I were a musician. Does that count? I'm so envious of the immediacy of it and the feedback loop that can build in front of a receptive audience. At least with live music, there can exist a purity of emotional expression and experience that I think most other arts struggle to achieve.

But to answer your question more photographically: No, not really. I'm interested in authenticity of voice. So, the more I trust myself, the more interested I become in my own ideas. The work begins to teach me about my own worldview. That being said, when I was a student, I definitely tried a lot of different things before I found what felt like a true expression.

7. How do you know when a body of work is finished?

It's usually when I start to get a little bored. And that's not to say that the pictures I've made start to bore me, but when I'm not curious or excited to go out to look for more. What tends to happen is I'll find myself pivoting to something else. Certainly, there are external factors like exhibitions or book deadlines, which can encourage a kind of finality. It can be good to have those types of end points, actually. They can keep you from becoming too precious about it all.

Potter

8. Have you ever had a body of work that was created in the editing process?

> To some degree I think they all are made this way. I mean, this is true at least as far as the audience is concerned. The editing process is a critical moment where the work takes shape and where meaning can be created through additive and subtractive gestures. I like to make small 4-by-5-inch prints of everything I'm considering and move them around on a table. It's important to me that it is done with real prints, because I wouldn't be able to see all of the possibilities on a computer screen. From there, I add and remove and rearrange until it feels right. It can take weeks, months, or even years.

9. Do you associate your work with a particular genre of photography? If yes, how would you define that genre?

> "Subjective documentary" is a phrase that gets used a lot around my work, and I suppose it comes close. Although, I can just as easily argue that the term is redundant. I feel as though I fit in among the grayer spaces of defined genres: I often employ a documentary language, I'm highly influenced by what some call Lyric Documentary (though I'm probably more conceptually driven than those artists). And I am increasingly comfortable with highly orchestrated pictures. Do we have a term for that yet?

10. Do you ever revisit a series that has already been exhibited or published to shoot more and add to it?

> Absolutely. I can think of a few times I've done this over the years, and it never occurred to me not to do it. *Manifest* was first exhibited in New York City in 2012, and I continued to shoot on that project for another three years. The truth is, I'm probably a slow worker. It takes time for me to settle with ideas and directions. I ruminate. I also seem to engage myself in work that often requires travel, which requires time and money. So, if someone offers an exhibition, and I feel as though I can put an interesting one together, I don't necessarily feel like it has to be an end point for the work overall.

11. Do you ever revisit a series that has already been exhibited or published and *reedit* it?

> Sure, why not? I really resist notions of permanency and believe my work can grow and change, just as we all do. For example, Light Work

[Syracuse, New York] asked me to exhibit my Gray Line series in 2017. That body of work [portraits made at West Point military academy during the height of the Iraq and Afghanistan wars] hadn't been exhibited for probably five years, and in the interim it had incurred a little internet fame and controversy. I felt strongly that if I was going to bring it back out into the public eye, I was going to do it in a way that reflected that history. I made a limited edition of ten pieces extra-large, to make them feel monumental, and I incorporated enlarged archived photos of my father's from Vietnam. The result was startlingly different from previous exhibitions, and I think it was stronger.

12. Do you create with presentation in mind, be that a gallery show or a book?

Of course I know those are options from the beginning, but I don't typically start envisioning either until I'm pretty deep into the work. I make small prints for a while before determining their final exhibition size. I pin pictures up in my studio and move them around; I start seeing how they speak to one another. From there, I make decisions about what needs to stay, what needs to go, what I still need to create or find to flesh out meaning. That's when the needs for exhibition and book start to really assert themselves in the process, and those two presentations don't always use the exact same pictures. That's what can be really revelatory to me, actually. Pictures that work in one regard don't necessarily work in the other. To add to the exploration, I've recently started working on some video and sound pieces, which I'm excited to incorporate into both exhibition and book form. ❶

"The pursuit of singularly great images is really at the heart of the daily practice of taking the camera out for a walk, but the greater and more urgent goal is to create a unique language of seeing . . ."

Gus Powell

First camera:
I hijacked my pop's folding Polaroid SX-70 to take pictures at my parents' parties.

First meaningful photobook:
The Family of Man (edited by Edward Steichen, 1955). When I was thirteen I found it at Strand Books. I had never heard of it . . . couldn't understand why a book with so many great pictures was only $2.

Gus Powell (born in New York, 1974) attended Oberlin College, where he studied comparative religion. His books include *The Company of Strangers* (2003), *The Lonely Ones* (2015), and *FAMILY CAR TROUBLE* (2019). He is a member of the street photographers' collective In-Public and is on the faculty of the MFA photography, video, and related media department at the School of Visual Arts.

First meaningful exhibition:
Bruce Davidson's *Subway* show at ICP in 1983, when the work was describing the present, but in Cibachrome. I had never seen red like that.

Personal fact:
If I could visit any city of my choice . . . it would be the street of Jacques Tati's film *PlayTime* (1973) with Giulietta Masina in tow and Roland Kirk leading the way.

Powell

1. What comes first for you: the idea for a project, or individual photographs that suggest a concept?

> It always begins with pictures that just have to be made on their own, each one for their own reasons. Most will never be a part of anything, but then there will be a picture that announces itself (sometimes at its creation, sometimes later as a surprise) as some sort of thesis statement, cornerstone, or riddle that asks for attention. That's the one that goes up on the wall that I use to inform my path forward. Other images will go with it, sometimes images not made by me, and also bits of language, an awkward title that is replaced again and again . . . and slowly the project emerges through a dialogue with that existing work, the making of more pictures that are informed by that dialogue, and then the editing and design of presentation.

2. What are the key elements that must be present for you when you are creating a body of work? (Social commentary, strong form, personal connection, photographic reference . . .)

> There has to be something that tugs at me as a true feeling, and there has to be ambiguity—the balance of those two, perhaps glued together with some humor. Tipping the hat to those who have inspired me is important as well, so references to such work are often there out of respect, and as something to stand on.

3. Is the idea of a body of work important to you? How does it function in relation to making a great individual photograph?

> The pursuit of singularly great images is really at the heart of the daily practice of taking the camera out for a walk, but the greater and more urgent goal is to create a unique language of seeing and to use that language to communicate something that is beyond a purely visual experience, that is beyond a singular image that is fixed to one time and place.

4. Do you have what you might call a "photographic style"?

> It's optimistic and "optic-mystic." Ever since I was a kid I have thought that being a florist would be a wonderful job. In college I majored in religion with a concentration in comparative mysticism. I would like to think my personal photographic style exists somewhere between these two ambitions: one seeking to reveal hidden truths found in plain sight,

the other serving up little made-to-order bundles of beauty from whatever is in season.

5. Where would you say your style falls on a continuum between completely intuitive and intellectually formulated?

> Often the stronger pictures are the result of an intuitive gesture, an urgency, and what could be described as a joyous expression that says "Yes" to something that is in front of me. But there is also an intellectual part of the daily practice. The "stronger pictures" have been earned/ gifted/cajoled after the making of many less successful "rough" pictures that are like preparatory sketches and often are more formally and intellectually constructed.

6. Assuming you now shoot in what you would consider your natural voice, have you ever wished your voice was different?

> I don't assume that I am shooting in my natural voice. I think that I reveal parts of my nature to myself as the work is being made, and with each body of work that voice changes a bit. Getting to hear and feel that evolving voice is a compelling reason to keep working.

7. How do you know when a body of work is finished?

> When it is an object that can go out into the world on its own. When it is something that could end up being found at a thrift store. When I can't remember it.

8. Have you ever had a body of work that was created in the editing process?

> *The Lonely Ones* [2015] was a set of orphaned images that I just did not know what to do with, and then I was reminded of a lesson from a poetry teacher of mine at Oberlin, David Young. He suggested that if you are struggling with what you want to say, choose an existing format with very specific rules, and work within that limited space. I had been obsessed for some time with the cartoonist William Steig's small book *The Lonely Ones* [1942], which pairs his line-drawn characters with dialogue-to-self, and so I decided to use the format of his book, both in scale and its use of text and image, as a form to insert and edit my work into.
>
> Similarly, my more recent project *Family Car Trouble* [2019], which is a reckoning with the arrival of children, the departure of a parent, and

the maintenance of an old station wagon, is completely dependent on how these three subjects, which I think of as three different sounds, come together through the edit to make a new sonic experience. It was completely conceived in the editing process.

9. Do you associate your work with a particular genre of photography? If yes, how would you define that genre?

I am most often associated with Street Photography. It's a genre that has no definition I am particularly fond of, and I can't say I have a definition of my own I am even happy with. With each new body of work I do I feel as though I move farther from making images that would be typical examples of Street Photography, and yet I think that all of my work has Street Photography in its DNA.

10. Do you ever revisit a series that has already been exhibited or published to shoot more and add to it?

Not yet, but I like to think of the poet Marianne Moore, who, upon the republication of her work, would often alter it each time. To improve it? To make it new? To mend it? Who knows . . . But it makes me think of it as a living thing, a breathing body, rather than a "finished" body.

11. Do you ever revisit a series that has already been exhibited or published and *reedit* it?

Not yet, but I imagine it will happen at some point.

12. Do you create with presentation in mind, be that a gallery show or a book?

The book is the format that I see pictures coming together in as a body of work. Throughout the process I make small layouts and even draw covers for projects that are underway—dreaming about that final form that the work could take—and even carrying these early crude printed maquettes with me in my pocket, as I try to move forward. Paper, a glue stick, and scissors are all important tools in my photographic process. ❍

Richard Renaldi

First camera:
Nikon F

First meaningful photobook:
Richard Avedon's
In the American West (1985)

Richard Renaldi (born in Chicago, 1968) received a BFA in photography from New York University in 1990. To date, five monographs of his work have been published: *Figure and Ground* (Aperture, 2006), *Fall River Boys* (2009), *Touching Strangers* (Aperture, 2014), *Manhattan Sunday* (Aperture, 2016), and *I Want Your Love* (2018). He was a recipient of a Guggenheim Fellowship in 2015. Renaldi lives and works in New York.

First meaningful exhibition:
The Treasures of King Tutankhamun,
Field Museum of Natural History,
Chicago, 1977

Renaldi

Personal fact:
I have a very large and growing collection of Pez dispensers.

1. What comes first for you: the idea for a project, or individual photographs that suggest a concept?

> For much of my career I have focused on specific projects. I think of an idea and execute it. Either the project develops sufficiently or eventually I drop it. I have nearly as many unfinished projects as completed ones. Sometimes, one project gives rise to another. For example, a portrait series I worked on for a number of years, photographing at Greyhound bus stations across the country, led me to attempt group portraits of strangers sitting together on public benches. Those images relayed themselves into a new idea, to shoot pictures of two or more strangers posing intimately with the stipulation that they must physically touch one another. This became the genesis for *Touching Strangers* [2014].

2. What are the key elements that must be present for you when you are creating a body of work? (Social commentary, strong form, personal connection, photographic reference...)

> I think it is important to be interested in what you are photographing, especially if it is personal work. Manhattan Sunday, my most recent series, which was published as a book in 2016, was largely based on my own experience revolving around gay nightlife in New York City starting in the early 1990s. It was both the source of my inspiration and an experience and culture that I still found invigorating.

3. Is the idea of a body of work important to you? How does it function in relation to making a great individual photograph?

> I love to make photographs regardless of whether they are part of a series or a random, isolated thing. However, creating photographs as part of a larger something, like a series or a photobook, is one of the attributes of the medium that compels me. Working under the construct of a theme or project can force an image-maker into scenarios where they are challenged to make unique or original single images that they might otherwise not be provoked to make. Single images can also function on more than one plane. They can be taken out of context and held to the standard of aestheticism or whatever other criteria might be present to judge their value, or they can function together in sequence to serve as pieces of a larger concept. The photographs should be strong in either case, but I think both applications are valid.

4. Do you have what you might call a "photographic style"?

> I really don't know if I do or not. I have many different projects, and I have shot each one differently. So, if there is an overarching style, we'll have to wait until I'm finished photographing to find out what it might be. By the time I retire there might even be some new terms! Therefore, I don't want to rule myself out of any future classifications by attaching to one prematurely. I do have a personal style though that involves cool T-shirts . . .

5. Where would you say your style falls on a continuum between completely intuitive and intellectually formulated?

> That is difficult to say since the source of creativity is a mixture of the two things, isn't it? I have been drawn to the visual arts ever since I was a kid. Though I don't think I knew much about "intellectually formulated constructs" when I was little and made a giant pastel drawing of Yul Brynner in *The King and I*. Nor did I know a whole lot about abstraction when I made a photograph of a cityscape using Trivial Pursuit cards.

> On the other hand, I had already learned about August Sander and Joel Sternfeld by the time I picked up the 8-by-10 view camera in 1999, and their work was in my consciousness as I began my own foray into street portraiture.

6. Assuming you now shoot in what you would consider your natural voice, have you ever wished your voice was different?

> I don't know what that other, different voice would even sound like. I know there are times when I see a fantastic image and think, "I wish I took that," or I'm so impressed by someone's photographic style or a body of work that I momentarily feel covetous of it. But at the same time I am usually happy to discover and enjoy someone else's vision. In general, I am content with my "voice." I've been fortunate to have had the opportunity to develop and nurture my vision over the past thirty-five years with guidance, affirmation, encouragement, and recognition along the way.

Renaldi

7. How do you know when a body of work is finished?

There are clues, such as when you start repeating yourself, or when you feel that you have said what needs to be said. Sometimes you might start to feel ambivalent about the project or distracted by something else. When that happens it might suggest that things are winding down for you. However, I think it is just as possible to feel "finished" with a body of work and yet leave the door open for revisitation. If the work calls you back, even years later, then there isn't any reason not to listen and reapproach it.

8. Have you ever had a body of work that was created in the editing process?

Yes. My last published body of work, *Manhattan Sunday* [2016], consisted mainly of exterior portraits and cityscapes prior to editing. It was during the editing process that I realized I needed to go inside the nightclubs. My editor helped me to reimagine the work as an entire night out, both inside and outside the clubs, rather than as page spreads consisting solely of exterior images.

9. Do you associate your work with a particular genre of photography? If yes, how would you define that genre?

I don't think my work is any one thing. From time to time, when asked to comment on the genre my work fits into, I'll have look on the internet to refresh my memory regarding how many genres are actually out there. According to a website I found, Top 15 Genres of Photography That You Need to Know, I shoot pretty much in every genre except "war" and "sports." Wikipedia has an even more extensive lists of genres, many of which I have never heard of, such as "femto-photography" or "tele-snaps." They sound intriguing.

10. Do you ever revisit a series that has already been exhibited or published to shoot more and add to it?

Yes, certainly. I've had opportunities to show a body of work that was still in progress. I know some artists prefer to work in a more secretive manner or hold their work back until it is completed. For me, I like to share, and I like to grow an audience for a project. It can take many, many years for some work to catch on with the public or find its audience. I think it is part of the whole process of finding a place for my work. I also use my website as a way of archiving, organizing, and experimenting with the images.

11. Do you ever revisit a series that has already been exhibited or published and *reedit* it?

As far as my exhibitions, I have shown several differently edited versions of the same body of work at different galleries. However, in terms of my books, I have yet to publish a second, revised edition of any of them. It really isn't time yet. Though I do look forward to eventually making a new edit of my first monograph, *Figure and Ground* [2006], should the opportunity arise.

12. Do you create with presentation in mind, be that a gallery show or a book?

Most often, I think in terms of publishing a book. However, I recently started doing installations created only for exhibition in a particular gallery or other specific location. Conceiving of and working within those parameters was an exciting new approach for me. ◑

Renaldi

"I gravitate toward the simultaneous presence of visual dissonance and harmony, an immediate atmospheric seduction that gives way to a delayed discovery of carefully wrought details."

Sasha Rudensky

First camera:
Konica Autoreflex given to me by my
high school boyfriend's mom, when I
was fifteen

First meaningful photobook:
Josef Koudelka's *Exiles* (1988)

Sasha Rudensky (born in Moscow, 1979) received a BA from
Wesleyan University (2001) and an MFA from Yale University
School of Art (2008). In 2013, she was awarded an Aaron Siskind
Foundation Individual Photographer's Fellowship, and in 2015,
she was nominated for the Prix Pictet. Rudensky is an associate
professor of art at Wesleyan University, Middletown, Connecticut,
where she is the head of the photography program.

First meaningful exhibition:
The work of painter Zinaida
Serebriakova, in Moscow, in 1988

Personal fact:
My earliest memory is very
photographic: I am three and twirling
in my parents' bedroom in front of a
mirror. The sun is streaming in, and
everything is golden, and I've just
found out that I don't have to go to
Soviet day care. I stare at myself in
the mirror and silently acknowledge
that this is the happiest I will ever be.

Rudensky

1. What comes first for you: the idea for a project, or individual photographs that suggest a concept?

I have occasional moments that bear resemblance to conceptual clarity, but those disappear the minute the grant-writing process is over and the real work begins. When I start to shoot, the acts of looking and seeing take charge and usually lead me away from cohesive ideas on paper and toward what looks right, or beautiful, or abrasive, or absurd. My best projects come from months of ambient shooting, which is frequently aimless and existentially frustrating, yielding few good images. It took years to recognize that all those rolls of film and trips across the Atlantic were not a waste of time and resources but essential to my practice. Because I am interested in history, cultural identity, and place (the latter defined broadly), the work requires a lengthy gestation period, ruthless editing sessions, and renegotiation of my initial assumptions of what is central to the project.

Ironically, the most organic project I have worked on was also one of the earliest. I shot Remains in my early twenties after receiving a grant to spend a year in post-Soviet industrial towns. My initial proposal to shoot in Siberia and the far North was scrapped once I realized I was setting myself up to shoot a narrative that has been done by many Western photographers before me: alcoholism, unemployment, and hopelessness in brutal winter conditions. Instead, I hunkered down in Moscow and devoted time to wandering in the hopes of finding that "something" that could be my own. I was partially saved by switching from black and white to color, and from 35 mm to medium format, as the necessity to own this new language helped to motivate the grind. After two months I made what I later called the "mother" photograph, the picture that in a potent way contained the facets of conceptual and formal ideas that shaped the series. After arriving at that image, however, it took months—if not years—to fully understand my process and to be able to verbalize my intentions in a nuanced and comprehensive way. Conceptual clarity is the last stop on the journey.

2. What are the key elements that must be present for you when you are creating a body of work? (Social commentary, strong form, personal connection, photographic reference…)

> I gravitate toward the simultaneous presence of visual dissonance and harmony, an immediate atmospheric seduction that gives way to a delayed discovery of carefully wrought details. Distinct use of light, immediacy of the palette, and controlled form of the frame are essential. Without those elements I have no picture, even if the subject lends itself to the bigger project.
>
> My visual language—the ambiguity of gesture, a reorientation of spatial depth, a melding of figure into space—are all highly formal, but where the form is not just continuous but indistinct from the content.
>
> Unquestionably, my work is also personal, though I rarely photograph people close to me and often photograph near-strangers. I am intensely aware to what extent what I am shooting is a projection of my own subjective and psychological response to the "reality" unfolding in front of me. In that vein, I have always felt a deeper kinship to Robert Frank's *The Americans* [1958] than to Walker Evans's *American Photographs* [1938], despite the strong stylistic disparity.
>
> My visual leanings are also strongly informed by the history of art, from literature to photography, though the reference generally does not take center stage and is there in the background, as a secondary layer.

3. Is the idea of a body of work important to you? How does it function in relation to making a great individual photograph?

> As much as I would love to be satisfied with the immediacy and freedom of finding singular great pictures, I have found it impossible, with perhaps Instagram being a notable exception. An ongoing project or a body of work is how I'm able to make sense of what I do, and the need to make meaning across pictures is inseparable from my practice. I am keenly aware to what extent that gets in the way of being open to great pictures, which are everywhere and independent of one's subject, and frequently mourn the loss of innocence that allowed me to have a polyamorous visual affair with my surroundings.
>
> The sense of awareness of what makes *my* work distinct, what makes a picture my picture, comes at the expense of being able to consume

Rudensky

more freely. And yet, I am still chasing great pictures, even if it is a handful, because without them I cannot justify a body of work.

4. Do you have what you might call a "photographic style"?

When I work on editorial projects photo editors frequently ask me to shoot in what they dub "my" photographic style, a request that is simultaneously comforting and confusing. It equates style with a wrapper that can encase an image, giving it a visual consistency and predictability. It also implies that one's photographic vocabulary is inherently independent and can be removed or added. As a result, I have interpreted the term "my style" very loosely, choosing to translate it as shooting in a set of conditions I feel comfortable in, in my case with natural light and pronounced color. However, that hardly gets at my deeper set of interests, and I have resisted using the term even in the context of teaching.

5. Where would you say your style falls on a continuum between completely intuitive and intellectually formulated?

Here the word *style* connotes methodology, as opposed to the previous question, where I chose to equate "style" with fashion. My working methods have evolved over the years. In my early twenties I subscribed to the pure and perhaps puritanical way of photographing the world as I found it, where the idea of construction was, if not blasphemous, then at least uninteresting. Graduate school—the influence of the likes of Philip-Lorca diCorcia, Collier Schorr, and Gregory Crewdson, as well as the very practical need to make work on deadline, which lends itself to a participatory role—gave me permission to make work in ways I found compelling, without feeling like I had abandoned the very thing that made me love the medium in the first place.

I want to simultaneously engage with indexicality and performance, truth and illusion, social document and fantasy, without the need to assent to a binary way of thinking.

6. Assuming you now shoot in what you would consider your natural voice, have you ever wished your voice was different?

> I doubt I am alone in admitting to having experienced moments of weakness, where I fantasize about making work that is in step with current fads of the market and the art world at large. If I am being totally truthful, I am very jealous of painters, who have a studio that can satisfy all their whims. But I am a photographer and am what some would describe as traditional, and know that I cannot escape my visual proclivities, which have to do with engaging the outside world with my camera.

7. How do you know when a body of work is finished?

> I have been wrestling with this question for the past couple of years because of my hesitation to let go of my last body of work, Tinsel and Blue [2009–18]. My inability to commit to finishing the old undeniably comes from fear that it implies a commitment to the new, which can be paralyzing. There is much solace in being able to carry on with what already has traction and rely on existing contacts and strategies. Deadlines can help as can discrete time frames. I did have a realization in my postscript trip back to Ukraine that what tethered me to the former Soviet Union, my sense of what is post-Soviet and how I have worked through my formulation of what that means, is no longer relevant, or not in the same way. The subject that has occupied me for fourteen years was generational, and that generation grew up and moved on, and I need to learn how to ask different questions. So maybe that is the answer—the project's underlying questions must remain relevant, because when they no longer are, it is time to let it go.

8. Have you ever had a body of work that was created in the editing process?

> I am currently teaching a class on photobooks, which has reminded me how complex and elusive editing is and how essential it is to the whole endeavor of photography. I am tempted to say that all bodies of work are made in the editing process, even if one leans heavily on a set of strict guiding principles during the shooting phase. As with everything there is a spectrum—there are the likes of Jason Fulford, who collects photographs without a strong sense of what the project is until the editing begins. That is not generally true for me. But I also like to cast a wide net that brings back a variety of catch, and it is in the continuous and

ongoing editing process that connections emerge, coherent thoughts are formed, and a "body" is created.

9. Do you associate your work with a particular genre of photography? If yes, how would you define that genre?

Any attempt to define a genre of art or philosophical affiliation is either too reductive or too general. For instance, the term "documentary" can imply a myriad of contradictory meanings, none of which are particularly helpful in pinning down or differentiating one photographer from another. I am an artist, and not a photojournalist, and as a result, I feel comfortable and even compelled to filter the world and interpret it.

10. Do you ever revisit a series that has already been exhibited or published to shoot more and add to it?

It had not been my practice to revisit series until the undertaking of Tinsel and Blue, which deals with the post-Soviet "generation" mentioned above that came of age in an ideological vacuum; the series has taken many forms, including several titles. Because of the scope of the subject, the years involved, and the ultimate ambition of its printed form to incorporate multiple discrete projects, I decided to return a year after my 2016 exhibition to fill the spaces of disconnect. The intense editing process leading up to my solo show at least partially brought to light what was previously easy to ignore and was an immense help in focusing that last trip. I anticipate that a book mock-up might have a similar effect, resulting in the need to continue to keep that door open for a longer time yet.

11. Do you ever revisit a series that has already been exhibited or published and *reedit* it?

Reediting is necessitated every time new pictures are introduced; the equilibrium is changed, and the process has to begin anew.

12. Do you create with presentation in mind, be that a gallery show or a book?

The concerns associated with presentation emerge in the mature phase of the shooting and editing process, once I have made enough key photographs to give shape to the ideas. My installations tend to be relatively straightforward and are an extension of photographic editing and design, rather than sculptural considerations. However, for the first time I have been working on a new archival project that is breaking with that pattern. Instead of treating the found photographs as images, I am playing around with pictures as objects, where the site, lighting scheme, and display will be essential parts of the concept. ❍

Rudensky

"I want my photographs to serve as an invitation to explore what is hidden, not what is shown."

Lise Sarfati

First camera:
Leica M5, given to me by my father.
And I borrowed my sister's Yashica
6-by-6.

First meaningful photobook:
Diane Arbus monograph (Aperture,
1972), when I was fifteen

French photographer **Lise Sarfati** (born in Oran, French Algeria,
1958) received her master's degree in Russian studies from the
Sorbonne in 1979. She worked as the official photographer for the
Académie des Beaux-Arts in Paris and joined Magnum Photos in
1997, where she was a full member for fifteen years. In 1996, she
won the International Center of Photography Infinity Award for
Photojournalism and the Niépce Prize in Paris. Her publications
include *Acta Est* (2000), *Lise Sarfati* (2004), *The New Life* (2005),
Fashion Magazine: Austin, Texas (2009), *She* (2012), and *Oh Man*
(2018). Sarfati splits her time between Paris and Los Angeles.

First meaningful exhibition:
I really do not remember. I was more
interested in wandering the streets
of Old Nice and the Port under the
blue sky and the sun.

Personal fact:
When I was thirteen, I would
accompany my mother who visited
lonely old ladies in bourgeois
apartments in Nice. I systematically
photographed these very old ladies
and their empty bedrooms.

1. What comes first for you: the idea for a project, or individual photographs that suggest a concept?

> I start with an idea for a project. The confrontation with reality, the encounters with the people and spaces photographed, is an exciting moment. It's impossible to rely on what is immediately visible to construct my series.

> I can't create a series of photographs without thinking about the exhibition of the work. Each project is different and requires a construct. Everything must be built within the context of the exhibition and how it will be shown. The construct can also include a book, but the exhibition becomes the controlled form with which one can establish a conversation with the viewer—a form of sharing.

2. What are the key elements that must be present for you when you are creating a body of work? (Social commentary, strong form, personal connection, photographic reference...)

> With a new project, I try to discover the key elements and hope that they will amaze me and be different from previous projects. I want my photographs to serve as an invitation to explore what is hidden, not what is shown; to leave the interpretation open to everybody, yet favoring what is very physical, very realistic.

> For the framing, I choose simplicity to show complexity. I try to concentrate on the inner movement of the characters. This might seem illusory, but it's possible. I feel the need for the final result to evoke a shift in reality, a sense of distance. The relationship of the body to its environment and of the environment to the body—this changes with each project and is translated in the image by the surface relationship between fullness and emptiness.

> I am drawn to the idea of floating in a deserted space; the relationship between the character and the void. It could be psychological, or it could be concrete. The viewer should always question what is more dominant: the subject or the environment. I've often met my characters in improbable places, on a street, in a bar, or anywhere, but they all had a connection: they had a feeling of voluptuousness and sadness mixed with a desire to live. The assertion of feminine identity is important for me. I like to photograph characters and women on the fringes, not because they are marginal, but because they displace the gaze. They

shine a light on history as it is written via the "extras" that no one pays attention to. It is through them that history is written.

Light acts like a language.

3. Is the body of work important to you? How does it function in relation to making a great individual photograph?

If I was a writer, I don't think that I could express myself with one word even if that word was extremely beautiful and mesmerizing. I opt instead for a series or a sequence. A series can be concise as long as it is situated in time and duration. The notion of time invested in a work is something that is important. For me, it is the proof of quality, of maturity.

I like the tension between form and emotion that can be discovered over the course of a body of work; the way in which photographs complement one another and interweave, creating analogies and correspondences. I think that the photographs resonate with each other to create a whole. That allows the viewer's perception to be sharpened.

I also want a form that is not dictatorial; a photograph should allow the viewer to have freedom to take an interest in certain details without being obliged to absorb the totality. I try to limit the heaviness of an overly erratic narrative where the viewer would feel trapped.

4. Do you have what you might call a "photographic style"?

There is a style in the choice of my interrogation, but I don't have what I would call a photographic style. To lock oneself into a genre or style is contrary to the nature of photography and limits the possibilities of expression. This doesn't mean that the theme of my photographs is unknown to me. I've worked on the topic of women and their image, their identity, in *She* [published in 2012], On Hollywood [2010], *Austin, Texas* [published 2009], and my earlier Russian work. *She* becomes a statement, where a woman with multiple faces asserts herself in her own familiar world; she is often a stranger to herself and her environment. Throughout my different series, I never cease to question the relationship between the individual and the outside world. In *Oh Man* [2018] I was swayed by the ambiguous sensation of the landscape— the attraction to the void and the enjoyment of space occupied by the figure, walking.

Sarfati

5. Where would you say your style falls on a continuum between completely intuitive and intellectually formulated?

> My work is intuitive and physical with a desire to share, but it is formulated intellectually once it is realized. Yet, at the moment I take the picture, I'm thinking neither about the intellectual formulation of my work nor about a concept, even if I know concretely how I am organizing and constructing my series.

6. Assuming you now shoot in what you would consider your natural voice, have you ever wished your voice was different?

> To try to use a different voice would be difficult. But I feel free to have formally different photographic styles.

7. How do you know if a body of work is finished?

> When I'm ready to install it in a specific exhibition space. To do so, I conceive of the installation using a model of the space and thumbnails of the photographs that emulate the actual sizes.

8. Have you ever had a body of work that was created in the editing process?

> Editing is a creative process. It corresponds to editing for a film. It is the decision-making selection process that creates a rhythm, either a temporal continuity or a discontinuity. All my series are created at the editing stage but also at the time of formatting the design and installation of a space.

9. Do you associate your work with a particular genre of photography? If yes, how would you define that genre?

> I think it's the historian and curator's job to define genres. I personally do not feel that I belong to a genre.

10. Do you ever revisit a series that has already been exhibited or published to shoot more and add to it?

> This has never happened to me. When a series has been exhibited or published I do not reedit it. I couldn't reshoot an old series because I wouldn't have the same approach or the desire to do so.

11. Do you ever revisit a series that has already been exhibited or published and *reedit* it?

> I've never done that. I'm more interested in springing into a new project.

12. Do you create with presentation in mind, be that a gallery show or a book?

> I create a series for an exhibition. That is the goal of any of my projects. When I'm working on a body of work, in most cases, I've already considered the printed format. ❍

Translated from French by Molly Stevens, The Art of Translation

Sarfati

"A photo project isn't like a novel with a final draft or a film with a final cut. There can be room for adjustment, improvement, and playfulness."

Bryan Schutmaat

First camera:
My first experience taking pictures was with the Kodak FunSaver camera, the single-use camera popularized in the '90s. I was always so excited to get the prints back from our local pharmacy.

First meaningful photobook:
I found *Seasons of Light* by Peter Brown (1988) on my mother's bookshelf when I was in my teens, and it made me think in new ways.

Bryan Schutmaat (born in Houston, 1983) is a Texas-based photographer who has won numerous awards, including the Aperture Portfolio Prize and an Aaron Siskind Foundation Individual Photographer's Fellowship. His first monograph, *Grays the Mountain Sends*, was published in 2013, followed by *Islands of the Blest* (2014) and *Good Goddamn* (2017). He received a BA in history from the University of Houston (2009) and an MFA in photography from Hartford Art School (2012).

First meaningful exhibition:
In 2005, I saw *Winogrand 1964* at the Cheekwood Museum in Nashville, and it blew me away.

Personal fact:
Between the years of 2001 and 2009, I played in seven different punk bands.

Schutmaat

1. What comes first for you: the idea for a project, or individual photographs that suggest a concept?

> I think for me it might be a little bit of both. I tend to begin with an idea, but an idea so indeterminate that it could hardly be called an idea. It's more of a vague desire to photograph a certain subject matter or geographic region. I keep the framework very loose, then narrow the focus as I proceed. After a few sessions out shooting, I look at the photos I've taken, and they reveal my interests and the sentiment I bring forth. It's almost like the work itself is in control and guides me to the next step. From there, I start to circumscribe the kind of pictures I take, choosing to shoot only what I think will contribute to the body of work that's gradually emerging. I hone the subject matter, the aesthetic approach, and I try to build an atmosphere with increasing specificity as I move along.

2. What are the key elements that must be present for you when you are creating a body of work? (Social commentary, strong form, personal connection, photographic reference…)

> I need to feel an emotional response pretty early on in order to continue a project. Clearly, a good body of work should be well-rounded, with social relevance, an intellectual ballast, strong aesthetics, and so on, but for me to think that what I'm pursuing is worthwhile, the foremost requirement is a strong emotional core. The work I'm making has to move me, and I have to be led to believe that it will move others, too.

3. Is the idea of a body of work important to you? How does it function in relation to making a great individual photograph?

> The idea of a body of work is crucial for me, and it gives me purpose when I go out to make photos. I think context has become increasingly significant, given that images are so ubiquitous and abundant in our age. Just about anyone can take a great photo, but singular images— as appealing as some might be on the surface—have a lot less value when they're not operating within a body of work to cohesively convey something meaningful.

4. Do you have what you might call a "photographic style"?

> Yes, I do. I'm not sure how to expand on this though. I like rural settings and natural light, and my work tends to feels very lonely.

5. Where would you say your style falls on a continuum between completely intuitive and intellectually formulated?

> The idea of an intellectually formulated construct doesn't appeal to me. My work is a response to the environment around me when I'm out shooting. As I said above, I value the idea of a body of work and setting out with a purpose or concept, but when I'm taking photos, I rely heavily on discovery, possibility, and what the world has to offer, so I guess you could say I'm closer to the intuitive side of the continuum.

6. Assuming you now shoot in what you would consider your natural voice, have you ever wished your voice was different?

> This is a really fascinating question. I'm not sure any photographer really has a natural voice. Photographers train themselves to follow their tastes and visual interests, and so much influence is funneled through every click of the shutter that it's hard to say what comes naturally and what is learned or imitated. I also don't think our photographic voices and styles are rigid and immutable. I shot large-format for years, but then I grew tired of how static my pictures were. I wanted more gesture and movement, so I did a short project shot loosely with a handheld camera, which marked a shift in my voice. Now I'm back to working on slowly composed large-format shots. Other artists and creative people do this as well. Bob Dylan changed his literal voice from one album to the next to save himself from boredom and to defy expectation. Experimenting is fun.

7. How do you know when a body of work is finished?

> What's the cliché? A work of art is never finished, only abandoned. With the kind of work I do, I could shoot forever, trying to improve the photos or tweak the edit or just fuck with things endlessly. But life is short, and at some point you have to say, "Ok, this is enough." If you feel the subject matter isn't thoroughly explored after the completion of a project, then you can always go shoot the same kind of stuff in the future.

Schutmaat

8. Have you ever had a body of work that was created in the editing process?

I'd say that most successful photo projects are "made" largely in the editing process. Of course what you shoot and how you shoot it is paramount, but making sense of that work and guiding viewers with a solid edit are also essential from my point of view. This analogy might sound ridiculous, but the act of taking photos is akin to farming or gathering ingredients. After you do a good job growing the food, you take those ingredients to the kitchen, and the editing process is like cooking. It doesn't matter how good you are as a farmer, if you're a terrible chef. I suppose in photo history there were some photographers who weren't good at cooking, but John Szarkowski did it for them.

9. Do you associate your work with a particular genre of photography? If yes, how would you define that genre?

I usually try to deflect these kinds of questions since all genres have their pitfalls. But, if pressed, I suppose I'd say I'm a documentary-style photographer who evolved from Walker Evans's approach to the photograph as "lyric document." In recent years, photographers working in this vein have strayed far from the traditional documentary practice in an effort to relay deeper expression and to affirm poetic truth rather than actual truth, which strict documentary ethics would impede. I think this is good for photography.

10. Do you ever revisit a series that has already been exhibited or published to shoot more and add to it?

The answer to this would technically be yes, because I've exhibited projects in progress. However, I thought of those shows as preliminary excerpts, knowing that the final body of work would be concluded later.

11. Do you ever revisit a series that has already been exhibited or published and *reedit* it?

I'm not opposed to making minor changes to existing projects. The second edition of my book *Grays the Mountain Sends* [2014] has a slightly different edit than the first edition [2013]. With books, I think it's fun to make each edition unique by having a change in edit, sequence, design, or materials. A photo project isn't like a novel with a final draft or a film with a final cut. There can be room for adjustment, improvement, and playfulness.

12. Do you create with presentation in mind, be that a gallery show or a book?

I think having the final presentation in mind can be very helpful. It guides your efforts and motivates you toward a goal, even if it might be nebulous at the time of shooting. For me, it has always been the book. I love exhibitions and big beautiful prints, but I shoot with the book in mind. Books have an enduring place in my heart, and I know the best, deepest experiences I've had with pictures have been with books. ◑

Schutmaat

"Bodies of work are like children growing up before you. It's a thrill to study who I was when these works were born and how we've changed each other as we've both aged."

Manjari Sharma

First camera:
Nikon FM10

First meaningful photobook:
Anna Gaskell (2001)

Manjari Sharma (born in Mumbai, India, 1979) received her BFA in photography from Columbus College of Art and Design, Ohio, in 2004. She has guest-lectured and critiqued at the School of the Museum of Fine Arts at Tufts University, Boston; Rubin Museum of Art, New York; Asia Society Texas Center, Houston; School of Visual Arts, New York; Pratt Institute, New York; Parsons School of Design, New York; and the University of Hawaii. Her first publication *Darshan* (2019) is forthcoming. Sharma lives in Santa Barbara, California, and Brooklyn.

First meaningful exhibition:
Kelli Connell, *Double Life*, Columbus Museum of Art, Ohio, 2004; *Marina Abramović: The Artist Is Present*, Museum of Modern Art, New York, 2010

Personal fact:
I'm a super messy mango eater. I'm usually cold and complain about it unless I'm taking pictures in the snow. I'm always broke until I get to an art book fair. I have a strong sense of smell and take shamelessly long whiffs from my glass of wine. I totally cry during the ASPCA Sarah McLachlan commercial—every, single, time.

Sharma

1. What comes first for you: the idea for a project, or individual photographs that suggest a concept?

   It is simultaneous. Sometimes an idea is strong, but visually you can take it only so far. Other times an idea is sparked by a visual, but it has to have longer, more investigative legs to give it complexity and depth. Generally speaking, I am intrigued when the visual has its seductive qualities but doesn't leave you in a superficial limbo. Instead, it's an invitation to dig deeper and find further satisfaction through the dialogue and conundrum that surrounds the picture.

2. What are the key elements that must be present for you when you are creating a body of work? (Social commentary, strong form, personal connection, photographic reference...)

   All of my projects stem from a personal connection, which I follow through with a visual strategy that echoes that connection. I'll have the germ of an idea, but then to feed it and make it robust, I have to act on it quickly. One of my favorite quotes is from John Baldessari: "You have to be possessed, which you cannot will." Ideas come and go all the time, but the ones that engulf you, sculpt you and refine your practice.

3. Is the idea of a body of work important to you? How does it function in relation to making a great individual photograph?

   Yes, the idea of a body of work is important to me, but that doesn't take away from the power of a great individual photograph. It's more challenging, I think, for bodies of work to have staying power, because the essence of the story is dispersed over many images. A single strong photo is like a one-person band, and it's not easy by any means to have one that is complete and memorable. But when you have many soldiers making up an army, each of them better bring something to tighten your troop.

   Bodies of work are like children growing up before you. It's a thrill to study who I was when these works were born and how we've changed each other as we've both aged.

4. Do you have what you might call a "photographic style"?

I think if my work, my lens, my palette, my compositions were to be visually dissected, I'm sure that commonalities would be found, but I don't have a repetitive identifiable look. I will say, however, that my photographic style is bound by the same inquisitive core that drives me as a human being, so what I see very clearly is the imprint of my mind binding through all my work. I also do enjoy collaborations, whether it's with one person in the case of *To See Your Face* [2015–15, with Irina Rozovsky] or a team of Indian craftsmen who created props, sets, prosthetics, and costumes for my project Darshan [2011–13], classical images of Hindu gods and goddesses. Collaborations give way to a very unique, altered iteration of your voice. Typically in art-making one is playing an instrument (or a few) all alone, and then occasionally a spontaneous jam session occurs. It's very exciting when working with someone else how you turn a note into an unexpected song. A song you might never have sung if you didn't have a partner to sing it with.

5. Where would you say your style falls on a continuum between completely intuitive and intellectually formulated?

It's always pure intuition that leads my visual plan, and then intellect follows suit like a good puppy. I say this because one is wiser and harder to define, and the other is an astute and analogical student. One can be synthesized into a bottle, and the other is like vapor. If I let the intellectually formulated construct lead, my work would start to look homogenous and boring, and to be honest, I can't. My intuition is too strong-willed to allow that.

6. Assuming you now shoot in what you would consider your natural voice, have you ever wished your voice was different?

I am drawn to others' work and have wished that I could nail a melody like that or wished that the notes in my series were arranged as exquisitely. Creating new work is an adventure that can be just as thrilling for you to discover as it can be for an audience. To hope for a different voice would be to wish for the adventure to be taken away. I feel I have miles to go before I sleep, and so when I experience a strongly willed voice that is slaying in its delivery, it makes me aspire for more and raises my bar, but, no, it doesn't make me wish my voice was different.

Sharma

7. How do you know when a body of work is finished?

>   The excitement in a project is deeply tied to the passion for creating it, and while a lot can be said about flitting in and out and abandoning a project too early, the same can be said about lurking in one too long. I know a body of work is finished when there are no angles left to explore, or when it feels like the images I'm creating are derivatives of my own work. Simply put, when the mind's belly feels full, you're done. It's important for me to honor that moment or else I feel creatively bound and enslaved by my own muse. Sometimes the lingering pays off though, so I think the answer here is to follow your own internal, abstract patterns of recognition.

8. Have you ever had a body of work that was created in the editing process?

>   I am photographing my mother as she journeys through dementia, and I've been documenting my family as her condition has unfolded over the last five years. This body of work has been emotionally difficult for me to shoot and share, as one might expect, but editing the work has revealed that the images are just as much about my father, who is her caretaker. The popular representation in Indian media is of a wife or a mother fussing about, overworking herself to the bone so she can nurture her family. It's not a typical sight to see a man, let alone in his old age, serving, feeding, and clothing his ailing wife. The editing process revealed that this work is not just about a cruel disease and its evident tragedy, but about who my father had become. While I was shooting, the camera acted as a shield, sometimes protecting me from really debilitating moments. In due time when I edited the work, it almost allowed me to discover hope . . . to see how that relationship between my parents was being reborn and also, contrary to stereotypes, that this is what a marriage or a companionship between two souls can look like.

9. Do you associate your work with a particular genre of photography? If yes, how would you define that genre?

>   While not always classically presented, my work is rooted in portraiture. I am interested in the experience of a person, their musings about their origins, and how they process and communicate the struggles they have been handed or have accumulated. It's what I would be interested in even if I didn't have a camera on me. Sometimes this takes the form of a personality-focused project; other times the story is tied to the objects and space, and the semblance of a person is implied. What

engages me is discovering how a person surfs the space between their given circumstances and their acquired experiences. This also means that while my impetus is clear, I don't neatly fall into a said genre. Sometimes I'm photographing a found visual, and other times my work is previsualized, sketched, and constructed. In all cases, however, it involves the presence of human form, for better or for worse.

10. Do you ever revisit a series that has already been exhibited or published to shoot more and add to it?

I've been making images of people immersed in water for a long time. Recently, during a residency at the Squire Foundation in Santa Barbara, California, I had the opportunity to expand upon an earlier project called The Shower Series. In its original iteration [2009–13], it was a series of portraits and audio recordings of people who shared moments from their interior landscapes as they washed themselves down with water. When the residency invited me last year to open the work back up, it was intriguing to visit something familiar, but for better or for worse, I was a different person, and while the work had conceptual overlap, it grew its own individual personality. The current work consists of portraits, audio recordings, a video installation, and projections, along with a performance. As part of the exhibition at the end of the residency, I projected videos of people in the pool back into the same pool, and then the subjects of those videos jumped in and swam along with their projections. This was a new space for me to explore, and it's been exciting to see the results.

11. Do you ever revisit a series that has already been exhibited or published and *reedit* it?

Yes, but form follows function so it's highly dependent on the body of work and my personal goals for it. As I've already mentioned, I've done this for The Shower Series. However, my project Darshan [to be published in a forthcoming book] was strictly conceived as nine images and is meant to stay succinct.

12. Do you create with a presentation in mind, be that a gallery show or a book?

Yes, I do, but then the work may also advise me and take me in a different direction. Earlier bodies of work of mine have been conceived explicity as gallery shows. In the case of Darshan, I saw their final presentation/destination being on a wall and that allowed me to make decisions accordingly. The choice of tools, size of prints, type of paper and framing were always considerations during Darshan, so as to previsualize and control the final rendering and experience of the work. In the case of The Shower Series, however, it's been more organic. The images came first, and exhibitions followed, but as I've shared above, it has been added to, and the new work has morphed into a new beast that also incorporates video installation. So, while I definitely also see The Shower Series overall as an exhibition, I can now also see it as a monograph in the future that shows how my work with water has changed over a decade. ◑

Sharma

Dayanita Singh

First camera:
An Agfa Click III from my mother who was an obsessive photographer and album-maker

First meaningful photobook:
The only time in my entire life I've stolen something was Robert Frank's *The Lines of My Hand* (1972), from the ICP bookstore when I was a student and couldn't afford the forty or so US dollars. Now I make images to make books, and I make books to make book objects. I could not have become an artist without that book.

Dayanita Singh (born in New Delhi, 1961) studied visual communication at the National Institute of Design, Ahmedabad, India, and documentary photography at the International Center of Photography. She has received numerous accolades, including the Prince Claus award, and has published sixteen books, four of which are from her own imprint Spontaneous Books. *Museum Bhavan* (2017) won the Paris Photo–Aperture Foundation PhotoBook of the Year Prize (2017) and the International Center of Photography's Infinity Award for Artist's Book (2018).

First meaningful exhibition:
The exhibition I thought to be so interesting that I wanted to charter a plane in order to bring one hundred photographers from India over to see it was an extensive 2005 exhibition on Robert Frank at the Fotomuseum Winterthur in Switzerland. It presented an overview of all his work—not just his prints—but his videos and, most important, his maquettes and books. It was not just an exhibition about prints on the wall.

1. What comes first for you: the idea for a project, or individual photographs that suggest a concept?

> It's a combination of both. I work very intuitively at the start (an intuition constantly honed by music and literature and conversation); I try not to put too many words to it, so as to keep the flow going. It's not easy because one can have doubts and I even may think I'm being foolish, but there is no other way for me. Once I have worked for a while, I get a sense of what the focus might be, but at the same time, I know that the work will only reveal itself on the editing table. This is the invaluable process I call "book-building." I think it needs a certain confidence as well as a readiness for failure, because what the work shows you may not be quite what you thought you were doing. Perhaps it is with time you learn to trust the work more than your own ideas.

2. What are the key elements that must be present for you when you are creating a body of work? (Social commentary, strong form, personal connection, photographic reference...)

> I must feel obsessed with a thought or feeling—not only do I wake up thinking about it, but I also start dreaming about it. Then I know something is there, otherwise it could be a passing fancy. Gosh, this sounds like being in love, and maybe it is! Then comes "go away closer," that need to be close and far away at the same time. I know then that the work is forming. Slowly, very organically, finding its own rhythm. Rush it, and it falls flat. It's often torturous, but I have learned to trust in this process.

3. Is the idea of a body of work important to you? How does it function in relation to making a great individual photograph?

> Making photographs is just collecting raw material, as a chef collects the best available ingredients for cooking. It is on the editing table that the work is realized. It may follow one particular thread or combine various cuisines. Or, let's say making photographs is like collecting words, so however beautiful they are in themselves, what matters is what you do with these words. Will you make a poem, a novella, pulp fiction, a film script . . . or leave them as magnets on a refrigerator? I find it helpful to look to literature for this analogy, until photography throws out its own varied forms. Making photographs is simply not the be-all and end-all. Far from it.

4. Do you have what you might call a "photographic style"?

> I think my style is to continuously go outside photography; to actually go deeper into photography you need to go far away from it, way outside it. Photography in itself is just not enough, and yet my questions, as well as my solutions, come from photography. So, it's not a simple relationship, I would say.

5. Where would you say your style falls on a continuum between completely intuitive and intellectually formulated?

> It starts intuitively and very quietly, a slow rumble, as it were. I have learned to give it my full attention, and I try not to wordify it. Later, the intellectual construct presents itself. It's not so difficult when the work emerges from your concerns, so in a sense the work is as valid as your concerns are. They may not mean much to anyone else, but to me it's the only way.

6. Assuming you now shoot in what you would consider your natural voice, have you ever wished your voice was different?

> It is what it is; I am lucky I found my voice. It may not be appreciated by everyone, but it is my own voice, so better I stay with it. I often say this to younger photographers—how long can you sing in a borrowed voice?

7. How do you know when a body of work is finished?

> In my case it never is finished. I photograph things I am deeply fascinated by, in a much deeper way than might be logical, so my projects are unlikely to disappear because I have an exhibition or a book.

8. Have you ever had a body of work that was created in the editing process?

> All the time. You start with one idea, and it is in the editing process that the work reveals itself. You just have to step back from that table full of hundreds of prints, and gradually something starts to appear, often quite different from what you thought you were working on. The unconscious is perhaps the most seductive part of photography. The skill is in letting it reveal itself; it takes time and a certain surrender. I always say making images is just 10 percent of the work; it is on the editing table that the work is really made, especially when the form emerges out of that process.

Singh

9. Do you associate your work with a particular genre of photography? If yes, how would you define that genre?

> The genre where an image is the raw material, and you build a form for it. I am not sure what to call that genre, but it's certainly the only way for me to work.

10. Do you ever revisit a series that has already been exhibited or published to shoot more and add to it?

> The exhibition is never the end of my interest in a particular theme or feeling. I am still photographing archives, after making several exhibitions of the work, the book *File Room* [2013], and even *File Museum* [2011]. My project for the *Carnegie International* exhibition [Pittsburgh, 2018] features more recent archives work, and I am in Italy to photograph the state archives here. Maybe no publisher will want another book of archives, maybe no one will want to show them, but I cannot stop photographing them. I never stopped photographing Mona even though *Myself Mona Ahmed* [a mix of photobook, biography, autobiography, and fiction, concerning the life of a eunuch in India] was published in 2001. I photographed Mona until she died in 2017, and even now, I continue to bring her images into other series; she will always be in my work. I only photograph what interests me deeply, and somehow those interests tend to linger. I think I will be photographing archives until I die.

11. Do you ever revisit a series that has already been exhibited or published and *reedit* it?

> All the time—the same image works differently in different contexts. I know this is not acceptable in the gallery world of limited editions, but I can be completely free in the book form. So the girl on the bed appears first in *Go Away Closer* [2007], then in *Sent a Letter* [2008], and then in "Little Ladies Museum" [a chapter in *Museum Bhavan*, 2017]. During the installation of *Museum Bhavan* she has even moved into *File Museum*.

12. Do you create with presentation in mind, be that a gallery show or a book?

> That would be like putting the cart before the horse, I think. I prefer the work to grow organically, without the limitation of the gallery or the book, and once I have a form I will offer it where it is suitable. But often when one starts you never imagine it will be suitable anywhere. When I made the *Museum Bhavan* images I could not imagine anyone wanting to show them, let alone acquire them. I made them for my house, as my own archive museum. ◑

Singh

"A body of work can reveal the nuances of a particular experience in ways that an individual photograph often doesn't have the room to do."

Tiffany Smith

First camera:
Minolta X-700. Still have it!

First meaningful photobook:
In high school I discovered a Robert Mapplethorpe photobook through a friend. It was in circulation at the library, and we would go as a group after school to look at it, immaturely giggling at all the "racy" content. I wasn't so much shocked (this was Miami Beach High, in the late '90s) as I was enticed by how images could be provocative despite the subject matter.

Tiffany Smith (born in Miami, 1980) is an interdisciplinary artist from the Caribbean diaspora. Smith received a BFA in photography from the Savannah College of Art and Design, Georgia (2007), and an MFA in photography/video from the School of Visual Arts (2015). She was a 2018 NYSCA/NYFA Artist Fellow in Interdisciplinary Work from the New York Foundation for the Arts. Smith is based in Brooklyn.

First meaningful exhibition:
The first time I recall being in awe at an exhibition was at Kara Walker's retrospective at the Whitney in 2007. I was most impressed by her sketchbooks, and how they displayed vulnerability, and how much power lay in that. Black women are rarely able to be viewed simultaneously as powerful and vulnerable in the public sphere despite, you know, being human like everyone else.

1. What comes first for you: the idea for a project, or individual photographs that suggest a concept?

> I'm pretty methodical in my approach and enjoy study and research so generally I start with a concept, research the topic, and form my project from there. I am usually attempting to navigate varied and overlapping themes so this process helps me to sort out my thoughts and determine my focus. There are times when I allow myself to create images more freely, for instance, when I travel home to the Islands and document my surroundings, but even that is preplanned and thematically focused—planning ahead allows you the room to be free.

2. What are the key elements that must be present for you when you are creating a body of work? (Social commentary, strong form, personal connection, photographic reference...)

> I am particularly interested in creating work that privileges the subjectivities of people of color, as representations of us are often generalized and marginalized by mainstream media. Working from that place, a number of elements come into play—social commentary, photographic reference, etc. My projects all carry some kind of personal connection to the subject—whether aesthetically or conceptually—usually with a degree of empathy gained from a related lived experience.

3. Is the idea of a body of work important to you? How does it function in relation to making a great individual photograph?

> I think that a body of work can reveal the nuances of a particular experience in ways that an individual photograph often doesn't have the room to do. That said, I think it should be composed of great individual photographs, and I believe as an artist you essentially make the same work in different manifestations throughout your career—in essence, continuing to contribute to one grand or overarching body of work.

> In my practice particularly, greater themes such as migration, displacement, and representation are explored through the narratives of specific subjects, contributing to a long-term project—like an anthropological study broken into branches of research.

4. Do you have what you might call a "photographic style"?

> I like to describe my photographic style as "a tropicolor melodrama in three and a half acts." I use pattern, color, and references to home decor elements and plant life as cultural signifiers that describe a ubiquitous tropical locale. These devices function as a tourist trap—luring the viewer in with a lush visual aesthetic to confront a commanding subject. Whether creating staged or composited images, or capturing more documentary-style photographs, saturated colors, patterns, and plant life are hallmarks of my style.

5. Where would you say your style falls on a continuum between completely intuitive and intellectually formulated?

> I would say it falls right at the apex, and that the development of my photographic and installation work has been symbiotic. The technical development of each helps to articulate the intellectual concepts I wish to address. But the way that I approach their construction is organic and intuitive—almost like translating a dream or vision. I absorb information about a subject and then sort of dream up how to depict it.
>
> In my portrait photographs particularly, I research and pull visual references from the diaspora—from West African portrait photography to African American vernacular photography. So in that way, the references are formulated through research.

6. Assuming you now shoot in what you would consider your natural voice, have you ever wished your voice was different?

> I think it took me quite a while to come into my full voice because it needed to be authentic. All of that is directly connected to my own personal development. I love who I am, who I was, who I've grown to be, where I come from, and where I'm headed, and I can't imagine what any other voice telling the same story would look like.

7. How do you know when a body of work is finished?

> When I find out I'll clue you in! Jokes aside, editing down is usually the toughest part. Moments endear themselves to me, and I want to hold on to them. I like to take my time with things; I like to eat slowly, to linger in the sun, I'm always the last straggler in the group at the museum. I view my work as an extended survey released in sections or volumes.

Smith

I don't typically shoot in a way where I approach subjects as a transient presence: I engage subjects that I share a deeper connection with. I try to find vulnerability in my subjects and hope to be vulnerable through the work, so on those terms I suppose it's finished when it's done.

8. Have you ever had a body of work that was created in the editing process?

I consider the work that incorporates photo-compositing to be made in the editing process. Otherwise, I make every effort to get a completed shot in-camera, relying minimally on post-processing. Editing/sequencing a series of images is always more of a challenge for me. It becomes difficult to be objective when you get attached to particular images or compositions. But the process of sequencing and editing is where a series really comes together.

9. Do you associate your work with a particular genre of photography? If yes, how would you define that genre?

Magical Realism.

10. Do you ever revisit a series that has already been exhibited or published to shoot more and add to it?

No.

11. Do you ever revisit a series that has already been exhibited or published and *reedit* it?

The bodies of work I've been developing over the past few years are part of an ongoing survey that I continue to return to. I don't reedit the individual images, but their sequence, when presented together, will change when new images are introduced. So in this context I will revisit and add to a series.

12. Do you create with presentation in mind, be that a gallery show or a book?

I tend more to create the images and then think about how they'd best be presented. To some degree I think about this as I'm creating the images, especially since I began presenting my images within installations, but the way that they're presented in that context is prescribed, so it doesn't necessarily change the way I would create the image. I continue to search for ways that I can present my images in different contexts and using different print media, so I'd say that the greater part of experimentation happens after the image is captured. ◑

Smith

"After I snap the shutter I never know if a photograph is truly special. Even months later I usually don't know. Great photographs are a mix of light, time, and magic."

Alec Soth

First camera:
Father's hand-me-down Canon AE-1

First meaningful photobook:
Summer Nights by Robert Adams
(Aperture, 1985)

Alec Soth (born in Minneapolis, 1969) studied at Sarah Lawrence College. He has been the recipient of numerous awards, including a Guggenheim Fellowship, and is a member of Magnum Photos. He has published over twenty-five books, including *Sleeping by the Mississippi* (2004), *NIAGARA* (2006), *Broken Manual* (2010), *Songbook* (2015), and *I Know How Furiously Your Heart Is Beating* (2019). Soth lives and works in Minneapolis.

First meaningful exhibition:
Jan Dibbets, Walker Art Center,
Minneapolis, 1987

Personal fact:
In high school I had a job delivering Chinese food and discovered the thrill of peeking into a stranger's home.

Soth

1. What comes first for you: the idea for a project, or individual photographs that suggest a concept?

> I usually start with a vague idea. But after the first exposure, this idea invariably is transformed. I'm reminded over and over again of William Carlos Williams's "no ideas but in things." By the time I'm done shooting, the original idea is barely recognizable.

2. What are the key elements that must be present for you when you are creating a body of work? (Social commentary, strong form, personal connection, photographic reference...)

> For me, the most important thing about a photographic project is creating links between the photographs without forcing their connection. I want to suggest a whole but leave room for the viewer to create their own meaning.

3. Is the idea of a body of work important to you? How does it function in relation to making a great individual photograph?

> For most of my career, the goal has been to create a body of work. I've always framed that in terms of the book. Great pictures almost felt like a lucky by-product. But in recent years I've gotten back in touch with the simple pleasure of trying to make powerful individual photographs. That's not to say I know what makes a great individual photograph. After all these years it's still a mystery. But that's also the appeal. After I snap the shutter I never know if it is truly special. Even months later I usually don't know. Great photographs are a mix of light, time, and magic.

4. Do you have what you might call a "photographic style"?

> If I do, it isn't intentional.

5. Where would you say your style falls on a continuum between completely intuitive and intellectually formulated?

> I've always thought of style as inevitable. Clothing is a good analogy. Even if one isn't concerned with cutting-edge fashion or "having a look," one invariably dresses in a certain style. While I may not be particularly concerned with my photographic style, I'm aware that I have one. I just don't find it particularly productive for my work to spend time thinking about it. So in that sense I'd say my style is largely intuitive.

6. Assuming you now shoot in what you would consider your natural voice, have you ever wished your voice was different?

> Yes. I'm envious of different types of photographers: people who carry point-and-shoot cameras every day [as opposed to an 8-by-10 view camera], people who photograph their families, etc. But I mostly try to accept that I am what I am.

7. How do you know when a body of work is finished?

> This is a difficult question to answer. If photography were a true narrative art like filmmaking or fiction-writing, you'd have certain narrative conventions like the feature-length film, the television program, the novel, the short story, etc. But photography functions more like poetry and, like contemporary poetry, is usually free-verse in nature. There are no standards for beginning, middle, and end. It's up to each photographer to create her own structure. In the past, I've usually used the book as the chief structural device. Since most of the photobooks I love generally have around forty to sixty pictures, that's been the number I tried to achieve. But I'm currently less project-orientated. Nowadays, I'm just happy to work on an individual poem and see where it takes me.

8. Have you ever had a body of work that was created in the editing process?

> This has never happened with a major project. But I've done some small zines, most notably *The Last Days of W*, from editing archival material. [Released in 2008, it includes work taken during George W. Bush's two-term presidency.]

9. Do you associate your work with a particular genre of photography? If yes, how would you define that genre?

> I suppose I largely fall into the genre that Walker Evans called "documentary style." But I don't want to feel limited to that genre.

10. Do you ever revisit a series that has already been exhibited or published to shoot more and add to it?

> No.

Soth

11. Do you ever revisit a series that has already been exhibited or published and *reedit* it?

> I recently republished *Sleeping by the Mississippi* and added two photographs. [First published in 2004, the book captures America's "third coast" through a mix of individuals, landscapes, and interiors.] However, these were added at the beginning and end of the book and didn't alter the original sequence.

12. Do you create with presentation in mind, be that a gallery show or a book?

> I almost always start with the book in mind. In recent years I've attempted to think more in terms of the exhibition, but I invariably fall back into the habit of constructing the book first. ◑

Soth

Mark Steinmetz

First camera:
My parents gave me my first camera when I was around six. I don't remember what type it was—sort of a toy camera, but it worked.

First meaningful photobook:
The Time-Life Photography Series, edited by Carole Kismaric, was something I looked at and learned from when I was in high school in Iowa.

Mark Steinmetz (born in New York, 1961) lives in Athens, Georgia. He graduated from Yale's MFA photography program in 1986, received a Guggenheim Fellowship in 1994, and has taught photography at institutions such as Yale University School of Art, Harvard University, and Sarah Lawrence College. Steinmetz has published over a dozen books of his photographs, including *South Central* (2007), *South East* (2008), *Greater Atlanta* (2009), *Summertime* (2012), *Paris in my time* (2013), *The Players* (2015), *Angel City West* (2016), and *Past K-Ville* (2018).

First meaningful exhibition:
When I was maybe thirteen or fourteen years old, my mother, who was French, took me to see a Brassaï show at the University of Iowa's art museum. I can still remember seeing his night images on the walls.

Personal fact:
I had my first darkroom around the age of twelve and worked as photo editor for my high school newspaper and yearbook.

Steinmetz

1. What comes first for you: the idea for a project, or individual photographs that suggest a concept?

> It's not so easy to disentangle my projects from the larger flow of my entire work. My photographic practice in the South and Los Angeles and Paris stems from my love for certain traditions in American and French photography. Some of my work has taken the form of tightly defined projects such as the little league baseball work, which became a book, *The Players* [2015]. (One afternoon I heard a bat strike a ball, and turning to the direction of the sound, I knew instantly that I wanted to do a project.) In turn, both *The Players* and a body of work on summer camps (to be published) stem from an earlier, more general interest in photographing childhood.
>
> In the case of the Angel City West series [later published as books in 2016, 2017, and 2019], I was young—twenty-two—and was exploring the vast city of Los Angeles in very loose, seemingly random terms; yet the photographs, considered as a whole, share many common themes, and the work feels purposeful.
>
> Most of my work has been about civilization in one way or another, but at one point I started to take walks in the woods with the intention of restoring myself. After the first walk without a camera, I saw so many interesting things that from then on I brought a camera and a tripod.

2. What are the key elements that must be present for you when you are creating a body of work? (Social commentary, strong form, personal connection, photographic reference…)

> There has to be a strong connection. I can't take even a tiny step forward if I don't feel pulled. It has to make sense to me, but maybe not in such a clear-cut, rational, and obvious sort of way. A lot of intuition is involved. In this way, I am taking a cue from Garry Winogrand and others. To my mind, *The Players* is similar to Winogrand's book *The Animals* [1968] in that both are centered on a spectator/spectacle dichotomy (separated by fencing/caging). I've just completed a project on the Atlanta airport, and Winogrand made a lot of airport photos before me. There are references to Walker Evans, Robert Frank, and Lee Friedlander throughout my work as well.

3. Is the idea of a body of work important to you? How does it function in relation to making a great individual photograph?

In bodies of work, photos are usually in service to a subject or an idea. When yoked together in a book, they have a particular sequence that cannot be undone. The intended spirit, the particular energy, cannot easily be altered. Individual photos, on the other hand, can be lifted from their original contexts, and their meanings can change with different usage.

I'm a little wary of the term "great individual photograph" as greatness is in the eye of the beholder. Many photos proclaimed as "classic" or "legendary" seem like simple crowd-pleasers to me. They're not so challenging. But perhaps there are archetypal images, which somehow strike a nerve and go deep into the collective psyche. I think it's wonderful if a photo transcends its particular body of work and becomes a focal point within the large tradition of beauty- and poetry-making.

4. Do you have what you might call a "photographic style"?

I like what Henry Miller wrote of Brassaï: that he had "normal vision" —the photos didn't call attention to any specific style. Brassaï himself wrote that the more the photographer tries to be transparent, to disappear, the more the photographer is present in the work. Nowadays, as I remain a black-and-white film photographer in a digital world, it does seem like my work has a look that is distinct. Film has its particular effects, such as backlighting as it skirts around the edges of a subject, and in general, I see a greater harmony among the objects. With digital, the objects within a frame feel to me estranged from one another. Everything is usually too cruelly crisp and sharp.

5. Where would you say your style falls on a continuum between completely intuitive and intellectually formulated?

I would say it's intuitive but disciplined. You look at the world through a lens and put it down on paper (and in my case it's silver black-and-white), and you place it within a frame. Everything has to add up. If something isn't helping the picture, it's hurting it.

We all live by formulated constructs to some degree, and it's hard to become aware of how they operate on us. I think there was some anthropologist's study a long time ago where members of a remote tribe were shown photographs for the first time; they had difficulty recognizing scenes and people they knew—viewing the world through optics and making sense of scale in a two-dimensional image is a skill that apparently needs to be learned.

6. Assuming you now shoot in what you would consider your natural voice, have you ever wished your voice was different?

I think I've been able to stretch the range of my "voice" over the years, but I've never wanted it to be different or to be more like someone else's.

7. How do you know when a body of work is finished?

When the energy supporting it subsides. This is different from fallow periods where patience is required (read Hemingway's *Old Man and the Sea*) or when I wonder if I'm just repeating myself and the possibilities for improving the body of work seem exhausted. Sometimes it's helpful to take a step back and try to see things in a new light. Oftentimes, I've approached what seemed to be a dead end when it was still time to persevere.

Near the end of a project, I might review it to see what gaps there are, which kinds of photos would shore things up, and then go through the contact sheets once again to see if anything is there. If not, then I'll go out to photograph what I feel is missing. I have a strong desire to "get it right," to make the project as strong as it can be. The body of work is finished when I no longer have this drive. I might be heading out to a shoot, but other things I see on the way start pulling at me.

8. Have you ever had a body of work that was created in the editing process?

Not quite. Editing can clarify and provide sharper outlines, but editing takes place throughout the whole process of making photographs. Framing the scene and selecting the moment when the shutter is released are editing decisions. I think, after the fact, editing can reveal certain themes you weren't fully aware of at the time of working.

9. Do you associate your work with a particular genre of photography? If yes, how would you define that genre?

> I wouldn't use the word *genre*. In cinema there are Westerns and gangster movies. Those are genres—they follow certain conventions; a Western probably will have a gun fight, a scene in a saloon, and a communal dance. There is also film noir, which is not a genre but more of an attitude, a mood—you can have Westerns and gangster movies that are film noir and even film-noir musicals. I don't think there are true genres in photography. There are places such as Paris or Los Angeles or the South that many artists have already described, so there is a lot of sharing of images about what these places are like.

10. Do you ever revisit a series that has already been exhibited or published to shoot more and add to it?

> I had a small show of little-league baseball photos at the Museum of Contemporary Photography in Chicago, and I continued to photograph a couple years beyond that. Now that I have a book, it's done.

> I continue to make pictures of Paris, modern Atlanta, cats, airports, and other subjects that have been published. Maybe this work will morph into similar but different versions of the original books. After all, you can't step into the same river twice because the river is constantly changing.

11. Do you ever revisit a series that has already been exhibited or published and *reedit* it?

> Some of my work was made over a long time span, such as *Greater Atlanta* [2009] and *South East* [2008]. There are certainly lots of other worthy photos from those time periods—and I'd be happy to share and publish them—but the book sequences themselves I'd rather leave alone.

> Nowadays with computers (and I have an assistant to do the scanning) it's much easier to unearth photos from the past. When I was younger, I couldn't keep up with all the work I needed to consider and print. Darkroom work is very laborious and time-consuming—it was harder to be thorough back in the '80s and '90s. Software programs today allow you to catalogue, label, and access photos more effectively.

Steinmetz

12. Do you create with presentation in mind, be that a gallery show or a book?

A gallery show is a special occasion, both for the artist and the viewer. It can be wonderful to experience an actual print, and in the case of large prints, you can see details readily and feel the work viscerally. However, I have always thought of myself as a book artist, though it took many years before I published my first book. I learned about photography through books more so than through gallery shows—I could keep the books at home and study them when I chose. For me, photography is a kind of literature, and is best shared by the book. ❍

Vanessa Winship

First camera:
An East German Praktica bought in 1981 to take photographs of my infant son. The pictures my partner and I had taken of him until that point had been mostly out-of-focus blobs.

First meaningful exhibition:
As far as exhibitions involving photographs, books, drawings, and sculpture go, then it probably has to be *Roni Horn AKA Roni Horn* at the Tate Modern, London, in 2009.

Vanessa Winship (born in Lincolnshire, United Kingdom, 1960) is based in London. She studied cinema and photography at Westminster University (Polytechnic of Central London) and has won numerous awards, including two World Press Photo awards, the Taylor Wessing Photographic Portrait Prize, and the HCB Award (presented by the Fondation Henri Cartier-Bresson). She has published four monographs to date: *Schwarzes Meer* (2007), *Sweet Nothings* (2008), *she dances on Jackson* (2013), as well as *And Time Folds* (2018).

First meaningful photobook:
Walker Evans at Work (1982). I bought it on a pilgrimage to London from Bristol to visit a photography exhibition at the Imperial War Museum and to shop at Silverprint/Goldfinger, which was *the* place to buy photographic materials. It was in Muswell Hill, a north London suburb. (We still own a Goldfinger catalogue. Product catalogues are throwaway objects now, but then they were almost like books.) More than thirty-five years later I still have the Evans book. Although the cover is yellowed, the work remains the same: truly wonderful.

1. What comes first for you: the idea for a project, or individual photographs that suggest a concept?

> I would say the grain of an idea comes first, and very often it's as a response or question about something. Then I try to be open to how the work develops and evolves, being willing to shift direction. I'm not necessarily trying to answer the question, but rather to find a way to visually express what I'm concerned with.

2. What are the key elements that must be present for you when you are creating a body of work? (Social commentary, strong form, personal connection, photographic reference...)

> Work that asks questions about the society we live in, personal connection, visually open pictures, enigmatic pictures, occasional photographic references, and, if possible, at least one note of hope.

3. Is the idea of a body of work important to you? How does it function in relation to making a great individual photograph?

> Although it is very important to have strong and visually engaging single pictures alongside some more conceptually based pictures, it's the body of work, as a whole, that's most important to me.
>
> Within a body of work, often there will be several strong, key images that stand out, which seem to carry more emotional weight; the challenge is to find a way to balance these images with the others, so that they don't lose their importance in the complete dialogue. You can do this by sequencing strong images that "speak" together. It's like building visual sentences, complete with all forms of punctuation. Or, imagine a piece of music where different emphasis is created using long notes and short ones, crescendos and diminuendos, along with moments of silence, which act as breathing spaces.

4. Do you have what you might call a "photographic style"?

> You could say that a lot of my portrait work looks a certain way. I make environmental portraits. I also make unpeopled pictures, landscapes, but these are sometimes a kind of portraiture as well.

I like to work in a very simple, direct, and mostly frontal way with the person I am photographing. I suppose after a certain number of portraits in this way, you could call it a style.

5. Where would you say your style falls on a continuum between completely intuitive and intellectually formulated?

If you were asking about a way of working during the picture-taking process, then I would say something like 70 percent intuitive to 30 percent intellectual construct.

When I'm piecing a body of work together, once the picture-taking process is complete, I begin by working instinctively, and as the process goes through a number of different iterations, I try to construct and deconstruct, also using my intellect.

During the editing process, I ask for the help of one or two trusted people; at this point I guess it becomes more of an intellectual consideration.

6. Assuming you now shoot in what you would consider your natural voice, have you ever wished your voice was different?

Retrospectively, I believe I was extremely lucky to have been brought up in something of a backwater place, and at a school that didn't have high academic expectations of its students. Instead, the school focused more on creative ways to achieve something.

I have an aptitude for most physical and practical things; I also have a musical ear. One teacher explained how he'd taught his wife to sing, and because he'd known her so well he was able to follow every shift and development of her voice. He observed how her voice changed once she became pregnant, and how it changed again after the birth of their first child. The voice is something living, and it evolves as we change and mature. I feel like this in the context of photography, too.

But, yes, it's interesting to try on another kind of voice; perhaps it's akin to feeling empathy.

7. How do you know when a body of work is finished?

When I start repeating myself.

Winship

8. Have you ever had a body of work that was created in the editing process?

Editing is pretty fundamental to how I put work together. I don't create work from a base of editing, but I know it will be part of the process further down the line. Once I feel I have all the images I need, I begin to process visually what the important elements are and which to leave out to strengthen and reiterate what I think I want to say. A very straightforward example is when I was making *she dances on Jackson* [2013], I'd obsessively photograph trees; they were so glorious. Obviously, I couldn't have a whole book of trees, or rather I could have, but that would have been a very different book. So I weeded, if you'll forgive the botanical pun, the pictures that were simply of trees in all their glory. What I was left with were trees that each had a different function in relation to what they might "say" or make a nod to. We all see things through our own prisms, so what I see and think I'm saying isn't necessarily the same as what you might see. Even then, it's not possible to describe in words—that's the point. Pictures aren't words, and they function differently, viscerally mostly.

9. Do you associate your work with a particular genre of photography? If yes, how would you define that genre?

I think it's become difficult to define genres, as the boundaries and lines blur more and more. The majority of my work is made by going out into the world, and is socially engaged, and due to this it can be both personal and global.

Photographically speaking, my influences are quite wide, and I'm constantly questioning how to best represent each theme or question.

10. Do you ever revisit a series that has already been exhibited or published to shoot more and add to it?

I almost never shoot more once I consider a work complete, but I often have more material than I need, which I sometimes will add to, and this also may take me into a new body of work.

11. Do you ever revisit a series that has already been exhibited or published and *reedit* it?

> Yes, certainly in the case of exhibiting work. Reediting something already published isn't typically an option; mostly it's a financial consideration. Usually this means moving on and sometimes you find a new home for some of the pictures that got left out from before.

12. Do you create with presentation in mind, be that a gallery show or a book?

> No, but I do create bodies of work rather than single images. I have to find a space or format that best delivers the work as it is meant to be read, in which one or more pictures are in some kind of dialogue. *she dances on Jackson* was made knowing there would be an exhibition and a catalogue at the end, so that was unusual for me. Almost 99 percent of the time the creation of the work is about the creation and not really the output. This comes after the fact. Whatever vehicle or venue the work will be seen in requires a different treatment and consideration.
>
> Returning to *she dances on Jackson*, the first venue felt tricky to navigate, at least for me, in that it was two separate long rectangular rooms with low ceilings. This automatically meant that I had to limit the scale of each framed image. The placement of the works on the walls was dictated by the sequence we created in the catalogue. For me, the book is the thing that remains; it's the constant.
>
> When I'm working toward making a book, I'm attempting to say something with the pictures, whereby one image speaks with or to another. If you're lucky or skilled you can create a whole volley of pictures that together begin to almost make sentences. It's like trying to describe music in words—how does one manage to do this, when music is so visceral? Words cannot begin to fulfill what sounds feel like, and pictures are the same. Some are totally silent, and some are noisy; some draw you in slowly and some you see straight away. So if you consider a sequence of images as a score, then you can begin to figure out the best way to go. It isn't necessarily a narrative as such, and it is often necessarily fragmentary. ❍

"If photography were a true narrative art like filmmaking or fiction-writing, you'd have certain narrative conventions like the feature-length film, the television program, the novel, the short story, etc. But photography functions more like poetry and, like contemporary poetry, is usually free-verse in nature. There are no standards for beginning, middle, and end. It's up to each photographer to create her own structure."

—Alec Soth

Index

A

Index

Index

Acknowledgments
Sasha Wolf

When I started this book project, it was a solitary and slow going experience. Then the Aperture team got involved and it was like a turbo charge. I am forever grateful to Lesley Martin, who has more good ideas and good sense than any one person should be allowed to possess. And on the occasions where we got bogged down, the steady-handed Samantha Marlow kept us on track with her super powers of forward momentum, uncanny organization, and sheer force of will. Susan Ciccotti helped make everyone sound their best, and contributed valuable opinions about the project all along the way. To you three women I say thanks also for being fearless artist whisperers. Brian Paul Lamotte, thank you for your great design, and for being so easy to work with—for understanding the project and accommodating my inexplicable love and allegiance to the color blue. Working with you was a dream. This book had the key support of Susan and Thomas Dunn. I asked for their help and they answered the call. I am so appreciative. Peter Kayafas, Matthew Pillsbury, and other dear friends, thank you for your early encouragement. And finally, a huge thank you to all of the people who contributed to the book. I asked for your wisdom, generosity, and honesty, in equal measure, and you delivered in spades—many of you, even before I had a publisher, which was a true leap of faith. I really am so grateful.

Acknowledgments

Colophon

PhotoWork: Forty Photographers on Process and Practice
Edited and introduced by Sasha Wolf

Senior Text Editor: Susan Ciccotti
Editor: Lesley A. Martin
Designer: Brian Paul Lamotte
Senior Production Manager: True Sims
Production Manager: Nelson Chan
Associate Editor: Samantha Marlow
Proofreader: Olivia Casa
Work Scholars: Charis Morgan, Madison Reid, Kelsey Sucena

Additional staff of the Aperture book program includes: Chris Boot, Executive Director; Taia Kwinter, Publishing Manager; Emily Patten, Publishing Assistant; Elena Goukassian, Copy Editor; Andrea Chlad, Production Manager; Brian Berding, Designer; Kellie McLaughlin, Chief Sales and Marketing Officer; Richard Gregg, Sales Director, Books

Special thanks: *PhotoWork* was made possible, in part, with generous support from Susan and Thomas Dunn.

First edition, 2019
Printed by Toppan Leefung Printing Limited in China
10 9 8 7 6 5 4

Library of Congress Cataloguing-in-Publication Data

Names: Wolf, Sasha, 1964- editor.
Title: *Photowork : Forty Photographers on Process and Practice* / edited by Sasha Wolf.
Other titles: Photo work
Description: First edition. | New York, NY : Aperture Foundation, 2019.
Identifiers: LCCN 2019018646 | ISBN 9781597114592 (alk. paper)
Subjects: LCSH: Photographers--Interviews. | Photography.
Classification: LCC TR139 .P565 2019 | DDC 770--dc23
LC record available at https://lccn.loc.gov/2019018646

To order Aperture books, or inquire about gift or group orders, contact:
+1 212.946.7154
orders@aperture.org

For information about Aperture trade distribution worldwide, visit:
aperture.org/distribution

aperture

Aperture Foundation
548 West 28th Street, 4th Floor
New York, NY 10001
aperture.org

Aperture, a not-for-profit foundation, connects the photo community and its audiences with the most inspiring work, the sharpest ideas, and with each other—in print, in person, and online.

Colophon